CANADIAN FIRSTS

Inventions • Sports • Medicine
Space • Women's Rights
Explorers • Science • Research
Arts • World Affairs

Lisa Wojna

FOLK
LORE
PUBLISHING

© 2008 by Folklore Publishing Ltd.
First printed in 2008 10 9 8 7 6 5 4 3 2 1
Printed in Canada

The Publisher: Folklore Publishing Ltd.

Website: www.folklorepublishing.com

Library and Archives Canada Cataloguing in Publication

Wojna, Lisa, 1962–

      Canadian firsts : inventions, sports, medicine, space, women's rights, explorers, science, research, arts, world affairs / Lisa Wojna.

Includes bibliographical references.

ISBN 10: 1-894864-75-1
ISBN 13: 978-1-894864-75-6

      1. Canada—History—Miscellanea. 2. Canada—History—Anecdotes. I. Title.

FC60.W63 2008   971.002   C2008-901163-5

Project Director: Faye Boer
Project Editor: Kathy van Denderen
Production: Trina Koscielnuk
Cover Image: Courtesy of Photos.com

We acknowledge the financial support of the Alberta Foundation for the Arts for our publishing program.

We acknowledge the financial support of the Government of Canada through the Book Publishing Industry Development Program for our publishing activities.

PC:P1

Canadian Patrimoine
Heritage   canadien

Table of Contents

Dedication

For Jada—may you always look at the world around you in wonder and believe in your ability to accomplish anything you put your mind to.

Acknowledgements

WRITING IS ALWAYS a solitary occupation, and for a book like this one—which required more wading through stacks of information than getting out there to interview people—the journey can feel a bit lonely. Having said that, the people covered here were eternally fascinating. I found myself spending more time reading about one subject or another, and a day would go by where I'd written very little, but I learned a whole lot. So to begin, I'm dearly indebted to each and every person whose story appears within these pages. Their efforts made a country proud. I know I'm so much the richer for learning about them, and can only hope these meagre ramblings help to make others aware of these amazing accomplishments.

Without the support of my brilliant editor, Kathy van Denderen, who managed to lasso all these many stories and reorganize them into a cohesive whole, and an amazing publisher like Faye Boer, whose skill I will always admire, this book would still be in the dream stage.

Every day I thank God for the family support I receive. Without my redneck husband Garry, who calms me down when I panic that this time I really will miss my deadline, I'm sure I'd spend way more time mired in worry than I already do. My children are always an ongoing source of inspiration, and one in particular, my eldest son Peter, keeps challenging me to expand my skills and try new things. My youngest, darling Jada, has contented herself to sit alongside her mama writing her own creations. And my parents, Mary and Mitchell Wojna, stand by me in more ways than one, and I thank them immensely. Without these dear people in my life, this and anything else I do would be meaningless.

Introduction

WHEN MY DAUGHTER went to Paris on a school trip, it was strongly suggested we attach a miniature Canadian flag, or some other equally recognizable Canadian symbol, to her backpack and jacket. "People in Europe love Canadians," we were told. One travel agent even suggested that folks who weren't Canadian have admitted to doing this. Somehow there's the perception out there that Canadians get special treatment—we're just so nice and all—just don't say so to a Canadian.

Really, if the self-deprecating lot of us who call this fair country home weren't so stubborn, we'd acknowledge that people everywhere love Canadians. And why wouldn't they? Canadians are friendly, polite, accepting of others and always ready to accommodate a differing point of view, happy to lend just about anyone the shirt off their back, always willing to say they're sorry—even if you were the one to bump into them in the grocery store aisle—you get the idea. But why? Why are we so darned wonderful?

Perhaps a little delving into psychology in general is in order here. If you follow one school of thought, we humans are a product of more than mere genes. We all are a part of what we've seen and touched and heard and experienced. Everyone is. And if we look to our neighbours to the south, we might be a little more objective in that analysis. We're neighbours sure, and we like each other well enough, but that's pretty much where our similarities end. Take how we look at our citizenry, for example. Why does the United States call itself a melting pot and Canada calls itself a mosaic? It has a lot to do with our individual country's histories, how our countries were formed politically, how we as a society have adapted to our unique environments, how we've responded to our country's first peoples, how we've dealt with civil conflict and war, and how we deal with religion. Everything has a hand in forming the individual personality, and it's no different for a group of people who walk under one flag and call a particular place home.

So what makes Canada, Canada?

Aristotle once said, "If you would understand anything, observe its beginning and its development." Canadians are often so modest that they pooh-pooh their accomplishments, if they admit to having any at all, and in the process do themselves a great disservice. If we go by Aristotle's quote, this only succeeds in keeping us from understanding ourselves.

In a way, that's what this book is all about—getting to know and understand who we are, what makes us tick as a nation, and above all to equip readers with the briefest understanding of some of our country's amazing accomplishments. Let me be clear when I say this is by no means a definitive collection of every Canadian accomplishment. Throughout the writing of this book, I learned a lot about Canada, and while I hope I covered most of our country's amazing accomplishments, I've no doubt missed a great many. Let me apologize, in advance, to all who have been excluded. Any omissions are entirely a result of my own ignorance.

In the meantime, enjoy what is here. Let your mind wander back to the time when Alexander Graham Bell invented the telephone, or the day the Canadarm made its first appearance in outer space. Picture the rugged shores of Newfoundland the day Leif Ericsson first landed. Imagine what it was like when, at the tender age of 15, Cecile Eustace Smith became the first female to represent Canada at an Olympic games. Go out and buy some Ganong chocolates, or indulge in a dish of poutine. And maybe, just maybe, after reading this volume, folks will start to stand a little taller, shoulders back, head held high, and boldly pronounce "We are Canadians. Look at all we have accomplished!" Okay, so I'm getting a little carried away. It's far more likely readers will smile to themselves, take hushed pride in our country's accomplishments and get busy creating more Canadian firsts that we can quietly celebrate.

History

The colonists lived in a world of wood. The pine forest was everywhere on the mainland; only Newfoundland had to make do with stunted trees poking up from the rock.

–Michael Bliss (1941–), historian and writer

LET'S FACE IT; history for most of us is dry and boring. It's about as entertaining as the laws of Leviticus—even die-hard theologians scan over most of that book of the Bible. But just as Leviticus is important, or it wouldn't be part of the Bible, knowing our history gives us a better understanding of where we come from and who we are.

The history of Canada is so vast that volumes upon volumes have been written on the subject. Some have focused on early explorers. Others have looked at our political structures. Still others have examined how our geography has changed from the time the first European explorer set foot on Canadian soil to today.

Deciding which stories to include in this book was difficult, and it goes without saying that a lot more information has been left out than has found its way in here. Still, there were a few obvious areas that anyone reading about Canada's historic firsts would want to know. For example, who was the first European to land on Canada's shores? Where was the first trading post, first settlement and first city established? When was Canada actually formed, and when did it become a truly independent country?

Those are the obvious questions about Canadian historic firsts. But this country's past is a lot richer than those rudimentary facts alone, and in many areas Canada has been a world leader. Check it out.

The First Explorers

The first inhabitants of this vast country we call Canada are believed to have arrived via the temporary land bridge spanning the Bering Strait and linking the eastern tip of Asia to Alaska's most westerly point, Cape Prince of Wales. But do we know who the first non-Native visitors to this fine land were?

The widely accepted answer is that it was the bold Norseman Leif Ericsson. Sometime around the year 1000 he led a group of explorers from the shores of Norway west through the North Atlantic. Spurred on by tales of a mysterious new land glimpsed from a distance when his father Eric first discovered Greenland, Leif was determined to get a closer look. The first place he landed must have been a tad disappointing because the barren landscape of what he called Helluland (Land of Flat Stone), which we now refer to as Baffin Island, looked anything but promising. But he had better luck a little farther south, first coming across the forested coastline of Labrador, which he named Markland (Land of Woods). A few days later, his expedition landed on the northernmost tip of today's Newfoundland, which Leif named Vinland, and he returned home with a ship full of lumber.

Although Leif himself never returned to this new land, his brother Thorvald and an entourage of 30 men did. Thorvald was anxious to set up a permanent settlement there, but then the group stumbled across a small encampment of about nine First Nations people. Not knowing what to make of the situation, Thorvald and his men attacked the Natives. All but one was killed, and that individual rushed back to his village and alerted the others, leading to the first recorded battle between Europeans and Canada's first peoples.

It was 12 years before another Norwegian expedition returned to the area, this time with a town's worth of settlers and all the livestock they'd need to establish themselves. The next year, Canada saw the birth of its first European baby when a boy named Snorri Thorfinnesson (or Thorbndsson, or Thorfinnson; no one is quite sure of the spelling of his last name) made his grand entrance.

Life on the Rock wasn't quite as smooth as these hardy Norsemen and their womenfolk thought it would be, and in time the Vinland colonies they established were abandoned in favour of life back in the Scandinavian countries. They continued to make expeditions to the new land, but made no further efforts at establishing a permanent settlement.

During the middle of the 20th century, researcher Helge Instad and his wife Anne Stine, an archaeologist, identified the site of that first settlement at what is now called L'Anse aux Meadows. By the 1960s, their efforts led researchers into the area where they discovered everything from homes and a bathhouse to a blacksmith's forge. In 1978, the site was named a World Heritage Site by the United Nations.

Other Exploration Firsts

- The next European discovery of Canada's eastern shores didn't happen for centuries after the Norse first visited. On March 5, 1496, John Cabot (Giovanni Caboto) and his sons were commissioned by Henry VII to sail the seas wherever they took them and seek out new lands. That first voyage ended abruptly, and though details are sketchy, sometime around June the following year Cabot reported spotting what most believed to be Newfoundland. He spent a month there and didn't return to England until August. Cabot, of course, claimed the land for England.

- It was Jacques Cartier who first named the country "Canada," misunderstanding the Iroquois term for village, "kanata." Cartier inadvertently made his first voyage to Canada in 1534 while on route to Asia. Somewhere along the way he obviously took a wrong turn, which ended up being a pretty good thing as far as the King of France was concerned because on that voyage, Cartier claimed the land along the St. Lawrence River for France. Cartier visited Canada twice more, was the first to explore deeper into the Gulf of St. Lawrence and the first to officially chart the St. Lawrence River.

- Tadoussac, located off the coast of eastern Québec near the mouth of the St. Lawrence River, was home to Canada's first European trading post. It was established in 1600.

- The first official settlement in Canada, and the first settlement larger than a temporary fishing village anywhere north of Florida, was at St. Croix Island. In the winter of 1604–05, Pierre de Monts and the 79 or so men accompanying him established a community on the small patch of land. It appeared they had everything they needed for survival, but the coldest winter in more than 100 years hit that year, ice floes prevented them from travelling to the mainland and almost half the men died. Still, de Monts' efforts provided France with a permanent presence on this new land, and the following spring, de Monts and his men moved to the mainland and established the community of Port Royal.

- Although land had been claimed for France a few times by now, Samuel de Champlain is actually considered the "Father of New France." It was Champlain who explored Canada extensively, pushing beyond the boundaries previously explored and mapping much of the land he travelled, eventually founding Québec City in 1608.

- The first explorer to navigate the passage between Baffin Islands and Canada's mainland was Henry Hudson. He made the journey in 1611. He was also responsible for discovering the "great inland sea" we now call Hudson Bay.

- The first missionaries to visit this new country of Canada were the Recollets, or as Native people called them, "Black Robes," after the black garbs they wore. The missionaries arrived from France in 1615 but weren't well received because they came with the attitude of pushing Catholicism on the Native people. In 1625 the Jesuits arrived, but they used a different approach in spreading their gospel. As a rule, they lived with the Native people in their villages, learned their language, were open to their way of life, and they offered to share their faith only when approached to do so.

- Acadia was first claimed by James VI of Scotland in 1621 and granted to a poet named William Alexander. In case you're scratching your head, wondering where in heaven's name Acadia is, you can breathe easy— your understanding of Canadian geography isn't as bad as you might think. Alexander renamed the land "New Scotland," or Nova Scotia.

- Britain conquered New France in 1760, ending what was called the Seven Year War. During that time the British army captured 69 ships. The French only captured six.

- The first war that the colonies of Canada, known as British North America, faced was with its southern neighbour, the United States, during the War of 1812. It was also the only battle between the two, a fact I'm sure we're all glad about. In 1812 the British emerged victorious over the Americans, winning for Canada the first step in discovering its own identity.

- Politically speaking, Canada was initially divided in two main sections, governed by the legislatures of Upper and Lower Canada. The two parts were finally united in 1840 under the Union Act, forming the Province of Canada.

- Henry Budd was the first Aboriginal ordained minister. He founded the first school in western Canada in Cumberland House in 1840.

- Almost three decades later, in 1867, Canada entered Confederation, becoming a federal dominion and signifying the start of growth toward independence from Mother England.

- The David Thompson expedition might have been the first group of white settlers to stumble onto the Crowsnest Pass, a particularly steep and dangerous area through the Rockies along the Alberta and British Columbia border. They weren't, however, the first to traverse it. That distinction goes to Michael Phillips, a worker for the Hudson's Bay Company, who travelled through the area in 1873.

First Canadian to be British Prime Minister

There aren't a lot of folks who've heard the name Andrew Bonar Law, and that's a terrible shame, because the man represents a significant first in Canadian history. Law was the only Canadian in history to serve as a British Prime Minister, and the "only British Prime Minister to have been born outside the British Isles."

Andrew was born on September 15, 1858, in Rexton, New Brunswick, a small, rural Atlantic village. Although Andrew's mother died in childbirth, his father, the Reverend James Law, with help from his sister-in-law Janet Kidston, took care of his young son. But when the Reverend remarried, Janet returned to the family's native Scotland, and after successfully arguing the benefits of taking the child with her, Andrew made his way across the Atlantic. At the age of 12, Andrew was cared for by three, distant male cousins on his mother's side. The men looked on him as their own child, and the kindness and concern they shared for the young boy resulted in Andrew acquiring the best education Scotland had to offer.

His working life led him to a career in business, which he readily excelled at, and while he continued to build his business and personal life—marrying Annie Robley in March 1891 and raising seven children—he also nourished a burning interest in the politics of the day. In 1900, Andrew Bonar Law was elected as the Conservative Party MP for Glasgow Blackfriars. For the next 20 years he continued to prove himself a devote, dedicated and caring politician who garnered respect from both sides of the House. His public speaking capabilities were held in high regard, a strength that landed him his first key government position in 1902 as the Parliamentary Secretary to the Board of Trade. Although Law lost his seat in the 1906 election, he ran for Dulwich in a by-election held later that same year and was successful in his bid. And despite ongoing health problems, on October 23, 1922, after already declining an earlier offer to take over the country's top seat, Law became both Conservative party leader and British prime minister. He served as prime minister until May 1923, when his health forced him to retire. He died of throat cancer in October that year, and his funeral was held in Westminster Abbey.

Although Law is often touted as "the unknown prime minister," having the dubious distinction of being the shortest-serving British prime minister of the 20th century, the title certainly wasn't a result of poor performance—his longevity in public office should bear witness to this fact. His name isn't as well known as it should be, but Andrew Bonar Law hasn't been completely forgotten by his native Canada. The community of Bonarlaw, Ontario, originally known as "Big Springs" and then "Bellview," was renamed in his honour.

First Scientific Dives
under the North Pole

Mention the name "Jacques-Yves Cousteau" and just about everyone in the world with access to a TV or a library has heard of the man. The late, great scientist of the sea spent his lifetime studying, exploring and filming the underwater world. But who studies people such as Cousteau and the effects that undersea exploration has on their psyche and physiology? Since 1962, Canadian scientist Dr. Joseph MacInnis has been doing just that. At that time, and throughout the 1970s, he began "studying the physiology and psychology of men and women working under the sea" and developing techniques for deep-sea diving in the Arctic Ocean. "Between 1970 and 1974 he led four scientific diving expeditions to Resolute Bay, 600 miles [965 kilometres] north of the Arctic Circle." On the third expedition, he established "Sub-Igloo, the world's first polar dive station," and in 1974 he led the first-ever, scientific expedition into the chilly waters of the North Pole.

After graduating with a degree in medicine from the University of Toronto in 1962, and completing his internship at Toronto General Hospital, MacInnis was awarded a Link Foundation Fellowship and began his studies in diving medicine. His work took him from the University of Pennsylvania to the depths of the Caribbean. But in 1970, Prime Minister Pierre Trudeau called him home. The country was looking at developing its first National Ocean Policy and they needed MacInnis' expertise.

Along with extremely cold temperatures, diving in the Arctic meant divers had to make their way under sheets of ice, posing added dangers to an already hazardous occupation. From there the firsts just started mounting one after another. Under MacInnis' direction, his team created the Sub-Igloo, and in the process filmed the first encounters with Harp seals and Bowhead, Narwhal and Beluga whales. His team was also the first to discover the HMS *Breadalbane* in its icy grave in the Northwest Passage. Crushed by ice, the British ship sunk in 1853, and MacInnis' team was the first to explore and film the wreckage. Considered the northernmost shipwreck known, it's located 104 metres beneath the surface and about 965 kilometres north of the Arctic Circle.

MacInnis was heavily involved in the 1985 exploration of the *Titanic*, and in 1991 he co-led a team in the filming of the first IMAX movie on the fated ship. In 1993, the good doctor also led the first research dives to the modern-day shipwreck of the S.S. *Edmund Fitzgerald*, which sank in Lake Superior on November 10, 1975, taking 29 men to a watery grave. In addition, MacInnis was the first to lead a team of researchers to a 19th-century mystery schooner thought to have sank in Lake Erie in 1870.

Aside from these numerous Canadian firsts, MacInnis has travelled by submarine into the cavernous three-kilometre undersea Monterey Canyon and made an even deeper descent (almost five kilometres) into the Atlantic, and he's explored underwater volcanic vents in the Atlantic and Pacific Oceans. MacInnis has also penned nine books on his various explorations to date, and is considered by many to be one of the world's leading undersea explorers. His work is widely recognized and has garnered him four honourary doctorate degrees, the Order of Canada, the Queen's Anniversary Medal, and the Admiral's Medal.

The African Canadian Experience

To say slavery in Canada was only a European invention would be erroneous. Some Native people took members from other tribes as slaves during times of war, a convention their rules of war allowed for. But they weren't treated in the way we usually think of slaves being treated, where their personal freedoms were denied, they were forced into strenuous labour and to occupy the poorest of living conditions. That kind of slavery was indeed introduced by European settlers.

The first person of European descent to own slaves in Canada was Caspar Corte-Real. He was an explorer who travelled extensively throughout Newfoundland in the early 1500s and was believed to have 50 Native slaves of both sexes. The first black slave purchase in this country was of a young boy named Olivier Le Jeune. In 1628, British Commander David Kirke brought him from Madagascar to New France, which is now Québec.

By the early 1700s, there were 1132 registered black slaves in Québec and 2472 registered Native slaves. Keeping slaves continued for some time, but in 1759 things started to change. That year, the first lieutenant-governor of Upper Canada (Ontario), John Graves Simcoe, facilitated the passing of the Upper Canada Abolition Act. This wasn't just a first for Canada, it was a first for the entire British Empire—but it was just a start. People were no longer allowed to import slaves, though the ones already in the country continued under the custody of their masters.

The last slave purchase made in Canada occurred on August 23, 1797, when Emmanuel Allan was sold at an auction in Montréal. In 1798, James Monk, Chief Justice of the Court of King's Bench in Montréal, declared the practice of slavery to be nonexistent in Lower Canada. Of course, not everyone agreed with him, but in 1811 the point could no longer be argued. Slavery was abolished in both Upper and Lower Canada and, with the passing of the Emancipation Act in 1833, abolished in the entire British Empire.

Before slavery had been formally abolished, Canada was already seen as an attractive sanctuary for slaves south of the border. From 1783 to 1865, when the United States finally outlawed the practice, black slaves were fleeing to Canada via the Underground Railroad. Among those escaping north was one Reverend Josiah Henson, a Kentucky slave who entered Upper Canada on October 28, 1830. It is believed Henson was the basis for the character of Uncle Tom in Harriet Beecher Stowe's 1852 book *Uncle Tom's Cabin*.

African Canadian Firsts

- Although not all historians agree, sometime around the year 1608, a black explorer named Mathieu de Costa is thought to be the first black person to enter Canada.

- The Anti-Slavery Society of Canada, a first of its kind, was founded in Toronto on February 26, 1851.

- Mary Shadd Cary established the *Provincial Freeman*, the first newspaper targeting the country's black population, in March 1853. Cary was also the first black newspaperwoman in Canada and North America.

- Although the first black person in Canada elected to public office is uncertain, one of the earliest on record was Burr Plato. He was elected councilor for Niagara Falls, Ontario, in 1886 and held that position until 1901.

- The first African Canadian elected a Member of a Provincial Parliament was Leonard Braithwaite. He was

the Liberal Party candidate elected to Ontario's Etobi-
coke-York riding in 1963 and served until 1975.

- The first black MP was the Honourable Lincoln Alexander, PC, QC. He earned the position in 1965, held a
cabinet position as Minister of Labour from 1979 to
1985, and was then appointed the lieutenant-governor
of Ontario, the first black Canadian to do so.

- In 1972, Rosemary Brown was the New Democratic
Party MP elected to the BC Legislature, making her the
first African Canadian woman elected in the country.

- Anne Cools was named Liberal Senator in 1983, making her the first African Canadian Senator in the country. She served until 2004.

- Stuart Parker took over the helm of the BC branch of
the Green Party in 1993, making him the first black
Canadian leader of any political party.

First to Develop Standard Time

I'm quite sure no one ever breaks away from the family nest with the quest of developing a new way of telling time. It's more likely that the ordinary individual doesn't give the concept of time much thought, except when supper needs to be put on the table. Usually it's not until you're in a jam caused by something as obscure as, say, time, that you give it any thought at all. And that's exactly what happened to Sanford Fleming. We can thank him for uniting the world on one clock, as he was the first to develop the concept of Standard Time.

When Fleming was a young man travelling through Ireland by train, he was stranded at a train station for a marathon 16 hours because of confusion revolving around the time of his train. Apparently a typographical error surrounding the AM or PM following 5:35 caused a misunderstanding, and the result was a long, long wait for Fleming. It was a situation that he would recall years later.

Sanford and his brother David emigrated to Canada from Scotland in 1845. At 17, Sanford had an education as a draftsman and surveyor, but he lacked work experience. Because the employers of the day wanted that experience, Sanford had to prove himself the hard way—on his own. He started out surveying and producing maps of different communities, some of which were the first of their kind. One thing led to another, and by 1852 he landed himself a position as assistant engineer for the Ontario, Simcoe and Huron line of the railway. Five years later, in 1857, he was running the show as chief engineer of the Northern, and then the Intercolonial Railway, and was plotting the route the Canadian Pacific Railway would make through the Rockies. For 35 years Sanford helped stitch this country together via the railway. And then he started thinking about that day when he was stranded at the station in Ireland, and he wondered how a train schedule could be better developed to avoid the delay he had experienced.

The first thing Sanford did was to examine how time was kept in countries around the world. It didn't take him long to realize there was no uniformity in this regard, which he believed was part of the problem. If communities around the world were setting their clocks based on when the sun was directly overhead, then everyone was marching to a different drummer.

Sanford's first attempt at regulating time was what he termed Terrestrial Time, which was loosely based on the 24-hour military clock. It was a start, but if everyone worked by the same 24-hour clock, noon would be bright and sunny in one part of the world, and dark as night in another. He returned to the drawing board, and this time, he was successful in developing Standard Time. Basically, Sanford divided the world into 24 longitudinal geographic regions with the Prime Meridian, or hour zero, set at Greenwich, England. As the sun passes over the centre of each region, clocks in that area are set at noon. There is a one-hour time difference between each successive region, but all regions strike the hour simultaneously. After presenting the system of Standard Time at the 1884 International Conference, several countries agreed to adopt Fleming's formula, and by the end of the 19th century most of the world had changed their clocks to follow the new method.

In the end, Sanford succeeded in uniting the world on one clock, and he also provided a method where his beloved railway could establish a schedule that wouldn't leave folks sitting and waiting for inordinate periods of time, at least not because of a typographical error.

Canada Becomes an Independent Country

Canada first became an independent country in 1867 with the signing of the British North America (BNA) Act, but it would take another 100 years before the nation stood on its own two feet. The BNA Act, now called the Constitution Act 1867, basically gave Canada a certain level of autonomy when it came to the business of daily government life. It united those parts of the country wanting to join as one Dominion and established a basis for governing those areas under one, federal, government. But the executive power belonged to the Queen of England; the Queen was still the head of Canada's naval and military forces and was still a Member of Parliament.

Total independence didn't come along until 1982, with a renewed Constitution Act, and though most of us know Prime Minister Pierre Trudeau was responsible for spearheading the effort to patriate the country, he wasn't the first to push the idea. Rumblings over the idea began as far back as the 1920s, and again in 1935 and 1950. During Lester B. Pearson's run as prime minister, from 1963 to 1968, those rumblings became a little more concrete with the "Fulton-Favreau Formula"—a formula for constitutional change that won overwhelming support from premiers across the country. That proposal died when Québec Premier Jean Lesage pulled his support in 1965, and it was back to the drawing board.

Perhaps it was only someone with the charisma of Trudeau who could in the end pacify all concerned. In 1980 he began his quest to "renew the Constitution," and he certainly had his work cut out for him. He needed to unite the federal government in the cause, and in 1981 the Supreme Court of Canada passed the Patriation

Reference ruling that all provinces needed to have their concerns heard and agree on the final document. In addition, the concerns of interest groups, such as the First Nations and the province of Québec and French-speaking Canada, had to be addressed.

In a vote of 246 to 24, the British House of Commons passed the decision to patriate on December 2, 1981. The following year, on March 29, the Canada Act 1982 received Royal Assent, and on April 17 Queen Elizabeth II herself visited Parliament Hill and signed the Act into law. Although the Canada Act 1982 gave Canada its sovereignty, the Queen remains Canada's Head of State.

Thankful Arrival

The setting aside of a Thanksgiving holiday is a North American tradition, and it wasn't, as many might think, first celebrated among the pilgrim settlers in Plymouth Colony, Massachusetts, in 1621. In 1578, Martin Frobisher and his entourage of European explorers celebrated the first Thanksgiving on the shores of Newfoundland. At the time, Frobisher and his crew were in search of a northern passage to the Orient, and found themselves in Canada instead. The first thing the crew did after they disembarked the ship was host a grand feast and give thanks for their safe arrival, marking the first European celebration of its kind in North America. The date for Thanksgiving has changed throughout the years, from November 6 in 1879, to finally settling on the second Monday every October, a Parliamentary declaration that was passed on January 31, 1957. The day was to be a "Day of General Thanksgiving to Almighty God for the bountiful harvest with which Canada has been blessed."

Settlers coming to Canada continued the Thanksgiving tradition that Frobisher started, but even this wasn't the first celebration of its kind in the New World. The Haudenosaunee culture, a confederacy made up of the Mohawk, Oneida, Onondaga, Seneca, and Cayuga people of southern Ontario and parts of the United States, had celebrated every year for centuries before Frobisher set foot on this fine country. Their traditional prayer was in honour of "The Three Sisters"—beans, corn and squash.

Other Seasonal Firsts in Canada

- The hauntingly wonderful scenes and sounds of a truly Canadian Christmas were first put to music in *The Huron Carol* (also know as *'Twas in the Moon of Winter Time*). Father Jean de Brebeuf wrote the Canadian Christmas classic, originally called "Jesous Ahatonhia" or "Jesus, He Is Born" for the Huron and Wendat people in their native language in 1640.

- The German Baroness Riedesel not only made her own three children happy, she made Canadian history. On December 24, 1781, she graced Canada with some of her hometown Christmas traditions, and erected the country's first official Christmas tree in her home in Sorel, Québec. It is commonly referred to the first Christmas tree in the entire continent.

- The first time Victoria Day was officially celebrated was on May 24, 1901. Being a country of strong, British roots, it's not a surprise that Canada has celebrated the British monarchy from time to time. A prime example of this is in our national Victoria Day holiday. Queen Victoria, Canada's first ruling monarch, was born on May 24, 1819, and reigned as "queen of the United Kingdom of Great Britain and Ireland and empress of India" from 1837 to 1901. Canadians celebrated her birthday during her entire reign, but it was officially declared a holiday in 1845, unless the 24th fell on a Sunday, in which case the celebratory date was moved to the 25th. When she died, on January 22, 1901, Parliament declared May 24, "Queen Victoria Day," and the holiday became a national one. In 1952, an amendment was added to the original declaration of Victoria Day, stating it would be celebrated on the Monday before every May 25.

- Alberta's first Family Day holiday was celebrated in 1990. After a busy summer and fall packed with holiday celebrations, the bleak winter months seem all that more depressing, especially without a holiday to look forward to. So that year the Alberta Provincial Legislature addressed the issue by setting aside the third Monday of February as Alberta Family Day to "recognize and preserve the values of home and family on which pioneers built the province." In 2006, Saskatchewan announced it was considering adding a similar provincial holiday, and in 2007, Ontario and Manitoba's provincial governments followed suit. On December 6, 2006, the Saskatchewan legislature gave its approval, and the province celebrated its first Family Day holiday in February 2007. Ontario also approved its provincial holiday in October 2007, and the Manitoba Legislature did the same in early February 2008. Ontario celebrated its first "Family Day" on February 18, 2008. "Louis Riel Day," chosen through a survey of Manitoba students, was the name given to Manitoba's February holiday. It was celebrated for the first time on February 18, 2008.

- Nunavut Day was first celebrated in 1999. Most people in the newly formed territory, with the surprising exception of federal government and North West Company employees, have been treated to a day off every July 9 since 2001. That's when all other employers adopted Nunavut Day as one of their annual holidays, a day set aside to celebrate the creation of the territory.

Other Historic Firsts

- Canadian James Puckle must have been a meticulous sort. More than 200 years ago he was the first to invent a gun that shot round and square bullets. Christians were to be shot with the round bullets, and the square ones were reserved for the Turks. (The few obscure sources recounting this strange first didn't state the reason for the differentiation.)

- Nova Scotians know how to have a good time. In 1606 they founded the country's first social club, the Order of Good Cheer. Life was pretty primitive and restricting in the early days of this fine country, especially during winter, a time that could be immensely depressing to European settlers used to the finer things in life. The settlers of New France had just spent a dismal winter at Ile-Sainte-Croix, and in 1605 they moved to a new settlement of Port-Royale, located on Nova Scotia's Bay of Fundy. The location was a better one as far as creating a settlement goes, but to make sure the quality of life would continue to improve, French explorer Samuel de Champlain suggested they establish an Ordre de Bon Temps (Order of Good Cheer). The idea was a welcome one, and in 1606 the club's first chief steward, Marc Lescarbot, formally organized what became the first, and is now the oldest, social club in the entire continent.

- Québec City, which was founded in 1608, is not only one of the first and oldest cities on the continent, but it's also the first one named to the UNESCO list of World Heritage Sites. The "Historic District of Old Québec" received the designation in 1985.

- Québec City is also the first and only walled city in the continent, a factor that led to its nickname "Gibraltar of America."

- Jean Talon, the "Great Intendant" of New France (or the only settled portion of what now makes up part of Canada) conducted the area's first census in 1666. The inhabitants of the new land numbered 3215, not including the Aboriginal population. Breaking that down a little further, there were 2034 men, 1181 women and 528 married couples.

- Paid mail delivery first took place in Canada in 1693, but it wasn't until 1775 that the country saw its first post office open for business. The post office, located in Halifax, Nova Scotia, opened its doors on December 9, 1775, just in time for Christmas. The federal government took over control of mail delivery in 1851 and first established Canada Post in 1867. It was its own federal department until 1981, at which time Canada Post was transformed into a Crown Corporation.

- The first European to cross North America was Sir Alexander Mackenzie. The explorer traversed Canada twice, charting the Mackenzie River and other waterways in the process. He wrote *Voyage from Montréal on the River St. Lawrence, Through the Continent of North America, to the Frozen and Pacific Oceans, in the Years 1789 and 1793*, after retiring to his home in Scotland. It was published in 1801.

- Sir Sandford Fleming may have been the man behind the development of Standard Time, but it wasn't his only invention. In 1851 he was also responsible for designing Canada's first three-cent beaver postage stamp.

- Canada entered Confederation in 1867, and the first official census of the newly formed independent country took place in 1871. Initially, The Census Act, established on May 12, 1870, mandated the first countrywide census be taken no later than May 1, 1871, and retaken every 10 years.

- Treaty No. 1, the first, post-Confederation treaty signed between European settlers and Native people, was finalized in August 1871. It signified an agreement between the communities of "Winnipeg, Brandon, Portage la Prairie, Selkirk, Steinbach, Lundar, Grand Beach, Emerson, Winkler," and other European-settled communities in the vicinity of these towns, as well as the First Nations communities of "Brokenhead, Long Plain, Peguis, Roseau river, Sagkeeng, Swan Lake and Sandy Bay." Basically this treaty, like others of its kind, required First Nations communities to surrender much of their traditional lands and, in turn, were granted "reserve land," the "present" of $3 per man, woman and child, and the promise of a school for each newly formed reservation. Earlier treaties dating back to the 1700s focused on issues of peace and friendship and, in some cases, land surrender.

- Manzo Nagano of Nagasaki, Japan, was our country's first, official Japanese settler. The young sailor stowed away on a British ship without any clue to its destination and arrived in New Westminster, BC, in 1877.

- Who was the first Miss Canada? The question is a little controversial, because there was a Miss Canada scholarship competition, which started up in Hamilton in 1946, and then a Miss Canada pageant, which ran for 29 years and first hit CBC TV in 1963. But back in 1923, another Miss Canada event was held during the Montréal Winter Carnival. Although unrelated to the others, the pageant nonetheless produced the country's first Miss Canada—Winnifred Blair of St. John, New Brunswick. She earned the title on February 11, 1923.

- The first Canadian to win a Miss Universe Pageant was Karen Baldwin of London, Ontario, in 1982.

- If you get right down to it, you can credit Canadians for first developing the American "greenback." In 1957,

McGill university professor Thomas Sterry Hunt invented the particular green ink used in the making of American money.

- Niagara's Horseshoe Falls has been a tourist draw since the first Europeans came to this country, but in 1960 it likely lost much of its appeal to the Woodward family. That's because their seven-year-old son Roger was tossed into the upper Niagara River after the boat he was riding on capsized, making him the first person to survive the fall. His 17-year-old sister made it to shore just six metres from the lip of the treacherous waterfall. The man operating the boat wasn't as lucky, and both he and Roger were sucked over. The man died, but Roger miraculously survived.

- The first national lottery to be won in Canada was claimed by a group of nine lucky women from Québec City. The $1 million jackpot ticket was drawn on April 15, 1974.

- If you've been to Vancouver's Gastown district, chances are you've stumbled upon Canada's—and the world's—first steam-powered clock, a tall and stately looking clock firmly planted on the cobblestone sidewalk. It's just as likely you have no clue as to its real significance, other than as a photo prop. As it happens, the Gastown Steam Clock is the world's only steam-powered Westminster clock. Raymond Saunders built the clock in 1977, using a design from 1875. It's powered by an underground system of pipes that provide steam heat to area buildings.

- The Shishalh People, who live off the coast of BC, were among the first Aboriginal peoples in Canada to achieve the right to self-government. This historic milestone took place in 1986.

Politics

Governments are like underwear. They start smelling pretty bad if you don't change them once in a while.

–Margaret (Ma) Murray (1908–82),
pioneer newspaperwoman and publisher

POLITICS. NOT EVERYONE'S favourite subject, and certainly not mine. But as I delved into the who, what, when, where, why and how of Canada, I found myself with not only a deeper understanding of this country I call home, but also a greater love for it. Sure, I studied this all in grade school, but trust me when I say that was a long time ago. Information not used is quickly lost, and I, like many other Canadians, sadly discovered that I lacked a firm understanding of the history behind the political formation of my home and native land.

Knowing the name of Canada's first prime minister is cool, and something that should run off every Canadian's tongue without much thought (it was Sir John A. Macdonald, by the way), but it was even more interesting for me to learn about some of the more unusual nuances of political life in Canada. For example, did you know that while Aboriginal people were granted the right to vote federally in 1920, they could only exercise that right under specific conditions, and those conditions weren't lifted until 1960! And you might be surprised to discover that one of our fathers of Confederation was the country's first and only victim of assassination.

What follows is only the smallest sampling of the famous firsts in Canadian politics—you'd need a library's worth of volumes to write about them all.

First Canadian Ruler

Canada's first prime minister, Sir John A. Macdonald, was a member of the Conservative Party and served two terms, from 1867 to 1873, and again from 1878 to 1891. Although the Conservatives emerged victorious the first time Canadians went to the polls, their victory was short-lived when the Liberal Party, led by Alexander Mackenzie, took over the helm from 1873 to 1878. Having tasted both political flavours of the day, voters reverted to the Conservative style of leadership in 1878. From then until 1896, a Conservative government ruled over the country.

Macdonald is credited with being a key advocate for Confederation. He saw the country as one whole and worked to realize that vision by purchasing Rupert's Land and the Northwest Territory from the Hudson's Bay Company. It was under Macdonald's leadership that the province of Manitoba was first formed, and he was also a huge proponent in the building of a national railway.

Macdonald was considered a maverick, marching to his own drummer and not at all worried about keeping up appearances—he was known as a chronic drinker. Still, he made an impression as this country's first leader and was voted as one of Canada's top 10 "Greatest Canadians" in a CBC voters' poll.

Sir John A. Macdonald was the first ruling prime minister to die in office, in 1878. The only other prime minister to die while serving as the country's leader was Sir John Thompson. He died in 1894 after serving just two years of his term.

History of Federal Party Firsts

- Canada's first federal election after Confederation saw more than just the Liberals and Conservatives squaring off against each other. The Liberal-Conservative party, which sat with the Conservative party in the House of Commons, saw 29 of its 32 candidates elected in 1867. The Anti-Confederation Party also ran 20 candidates and, under the party leadership of Joseph Howe, saw 18 of their members elected. In Parliament, the Anti-Confederation Party sat with the Liberal Party. Several strains of independent candidates also ran, but none was elected.

- The federal New Democratic Party (NDP) first came onto the political radar in 1961 when, at their founding convention, Tommy Douglas emerged as its first leader. Douglas, a strong proponent of the social gospel, was deeply affected by the suffering he'd witnessed during and after the Great Depression. Initially he focused his efforts as a member of the Independent Labour Party— a party whose roots date back to the 1870s. But it wasn't until his involvement with the Co-operative Commonwealth Federation (CCF) and his run as a candidate for Saskatchewan in the 1935 election that he landed a seat in the House of Commons. He bounced between provincial and federal politics, but with his newfound leadership of the NDP, Douglas made perhaps his biggest mark on the country when in 1971 he advocated for a national medical system (Medicare), Canada Pension and "the expansion of Canada's social safety net." In a 2004, CBC poll, Douglas was voted our nation's Greatest Canadian.

First Political Assassination

Born in Carlingford, Ireland, on April 13, 1825, Thomas D'Arcy McGee came into the world at a time when political upheaval was present everywhere. In the Ireland of McGee's day, Catholics were looking for emancipation from the penal laws imposed on them since the mid-1600s. In the New World of the Americas, land was just being settled and boundaries erected.

At the age of 17 McGee immigrated to the U.S. and put his writing skills to use as an assistant editor at the Catholic newspaper, *Boston Pilot*. Although his tenure there was successful, the land of his birth called him home, and McGee became politically involved in the Irish nationalist movement. Eventually, he returned to the U.S., fleeing from a warrant for his arrest for his involvement in the Young Irelander Rebellion of 1848. In doing so he brought his political views to the Irish living in the New World. He was so passionate an orator—blending his writing skills with his love of poetry—that although he drew some negative attention from church leaders of the day, he also gained admiration from Irish nationalists in Canada. By 1857 he had crossed the border to set up a life for himself in Montréal.

In December 1858, McGee landed a seat in the Legislative Assembly of the Province of Canada. "I see in the not remote distance one great nationality bound like the shield of Achilles, by the blue rim of ocean...I see within the ground of that shield the peaks of the western mountains and the crests of the eastern waves." He delivered those words in 1860, and in doing so rallied for a new Canadian nationality. Although he once supported American annexation, he was a strong advocate for Confederation and the building of a national railway. He sat at the table at both the Charlottetown and Québec Conference, and two speeches he delivered in 1865 on the union of the provinces were published.

In the general election of 1867, McGee once again won his seat, and his signature on the newly formed BNA Act secured his place in history as one of Canada's fathers of Confederation. His popularity had faded somewhat, and he was considering a life outside of politics, when on April 7, 1868, McGee delivered another speech supporting national unity from the floor of the House of Commons. As usual, his words pumped life and energy into the late-night session, but not everyone agreed with his sentiments. While walking to his home on Ottawa's Sparks Street that night, McGee was shot and killed, giving him the ominous distinction of being Canada's one and only victim of political assassination.

In 1869, Patrick James Whalen was found guilty and hanged for the murder.

First Woman Elected
as a Member of Parliament

Probably the two best words to describe Agnes Campbell Macphail are "activist" and "philanthropist." Born to
a farming family in Ontario in 1890, she understood
from a young age what it meant to be impoverished—she
saw it firsthand. But instead of closing her mind to the
problem, Agnes sprang into action. As a young schoolteacher she'd already spoken out on social justice issues,
and it was that outspokenness that led her to a position in
federal politics.

When first elected as the federal member for Ontario's
Grey County in 1921, she not only propelled herself into
a position of influence but also made history as the first
woman elected to the federal government. Her male colleagues were less than impressed with her presence in
the House of Commons. Even Tommy Douglas once com-
mented she was "about as welcome…as a skunk at a gar-
den party." The less-than-warm reception might have
softened another woman's resolve, but not Macphail's.
She went on to serve her constituents for 19 years before
eventually losing her seat in the 1940 election.

In 1929, Macphail became the first Canadian woman
to sit as a delegate at the League of Nations in Geneva,
Switzerland. She also served as the first president of the
Ontario CCF, accepting the position in 1933. And in 1939,
she founded the Elizabeth Fry Society of Canada. She
died, penniless, in 1954. She had given most of what she
had to the poor.

First Woman Elected Leader of a Federal Party

Born on November 7, 1936, in Dutton, Ontario, Audrey McLaughlin was the first in her family to earn a university degree. By the time she was elected as an NDP Member of Parliament for the Yukon in 1987, she'd worked as a teacher in Ghana, West Africa, and as a social worker with Children's Aid Society of Metropolitan Toronto. Her election was a first for the NDP since no other federal NDP candidate had secured a seat in the Yukon. Just two years later, McLaughlin clocked another political first when she competed in the leadership race to replace Ed Broadbent, and on December 2, 1989, she became the first woman elected leader of a federal political party in Canada.

When Audrey McLaughlin took over, the federal NDP was at its height of popularity, but that was about to change. In British Columbia and Ontario, the provincial arms of the NDP were struggling, and that reflected on the popularity of the federal NDP. During McLaughlin's leadership the party struggled, and although she maintained her seat in the 1993 general election, her party only garnered nine seats in the House of Commons. She resigned in April 1994, and Alexa McDonough succeeded her as leader of the party at the NDP convention in October 1995.

Firsts for the Green Party

Although the Green Party of Canada doesn't hold a single seat in the House of Commons, with about 9000 registered members, it's the largest federal party without one. Founded in 1983, the party focuses its policies on six guiding principles: ecological wisdom, social justice, participatory democracy, nonviolence, sustainability and respect for diversity. It's the first political party to launch a "mass rejection of consumer culture" and to campaign on that platform—not always popular in an increasingly materialistic world.

Sixty candidates campaigned in the 1984 federal election under the party's first leader, Dr. Trevor Hancock. It was a slow start, but the Greens continue to increase the number of candidates they run, and in 2004, they became only the "fourth federal political party ever to run candidates in all 308 ridings." When the ballots were counted, it was clear they still hadn't captured a seat on Parliament Hill, but their popular vote had risen to 4.3 percent, giving them the minimum two percent required to elicit financing under the rules governing elections in the country.

The first woman elected as federal Green Party leader was Kathryn Cholette. She served from 1988 to 1990. Elizabeth May is the party's current leader. She was elected in 2006, and when she ran in the riding of London North Centre by-election, she stunned the media by coming in with a second-place finish against her opponents and earning 25.8 percent of the vote—a best-ever Green Party result.

Other Political Firsts

- King Francis I was the first king to rule over this vast land for France. He ruled the area from 1534 to 1763. From the first official exploration into this country we call Canada, we've been under the rule of a monarch. Canada's first British monarch was King George III. He ruled from 1763 to 1820.

- Ezekiel Hart was the first Jewish Canadian elected to a Legislature, earning that honour on April 11, 1807, when he won a Lower Canada by-election. Jewish Canadians weren't given full political rights in Lower Canada until 1831, more than 20 years later.

- The first election held in what was then the Province of Canada took place in 1841. The two parties, called the reformers, made up of the Reform party in the West (29 seats) and Patriots in the East (21 seats), formed that first government. These reformers purported left wing and pro-democratic views. The conservative parties of the day, Family Compact in the West (10 seats) and Tories in the East (17 seats), were on the right wing of the new government, and the nonaligned independent parties took five seats altogether. There were a total of eight elections before Confederation, the last one taking place in 1863. That last election saw the Liberal Party of the day emerging victorious with 66 seats; the Conservative Party came in second with 35 seats; the more moderate parties of the Reform and Bleu took 27 seats; and the Independents had one seat.

- Canada's first election as a new nation ran from August 7 to September 20, 1867. There were 181 seats in the House of Commons at the time, and our country has returned to the polls another 37 times since then.

- The first four provinces to enter Confederation in 1867 were Ontario, Québec, Nova Scotia and New Brunswick. Manitoba was the fifth province to sign on with the deal in 1870, followed by British Columbia in 1871, Prince Edward Island in 1873, Yukon Territory in 1898, Alberta and Saskatchewan in 1905, Newfoundland in 1949 and Nunavut in 1999.

- Henry Nathan was the first Jewish person elected to the House of Commons, and he served in the capacity for two years. He was elected Liberal Party MP for Victoria in 1872.

- The country's second prime minister, Alexander Mackenzie, was the first to introduce the secret ballot, a method of voting where MPs are guaranteed voting confidentiality, into the Canadian House of Commons in 1874.

- The first province to grant women the right to vote was Manitoba. Thanks to the efforts of suffragettes such as Nellie McClung, Manitoba politicians saw the light of day in 1916.

- In 1917, Louise McKinney made history when she was elected as a member of the Alberta Legislature—she was the first woman in the country and the entire British Empire to be elected to such a position.

- Also in 1917, Mary Ellen Spear Smith was the first woman elected to the BC Legislature, campaigning to succeed her husband who died suddenly that year. Her election was an accomplishment she bettered twice over when in 1921 she became BC's first female cabinet minister, the first cabinet minister anywhere in the Western world, and then again when she became the first woman speaker in the entire British Empire.

- Hannah Gale made Canadian history on December 10, 1917, when she became the first woman elected to any political body in Canada. She was elected as an alderman in Calgary's city council. She served in that position until 1923.

- Women cast election ballots in a federal election in Canada for the first time in 1918, after winning the right to vote. Strangely enough, they still weren't classified as "persons" under Canadian law until 1929.

- Canada's first chief electoral officer was a retired army colonel named Mowat Biggar. The House of Commons appointed him to the position in 1920, and he continued to serve until 1927. And in case you were wondering, a chief electoral officer has numerous responsibilities, but the most important among them is ensuring that every eligible person in the country has a chance to vote.

- Aboriginal people could vote as early as 1920, but they had to relinquish their treaty rights and status to do so. These conditions weren't lifted until 1960!

- The first woman to be named to the Canadian Senate was Cairine Wilson. She filled a vacant seat in 1930.

- In 1936, Barbara Hanley was voted mayor of Webbwood, Ontario, making her the first woman in Canada to hold that position.

- It wasn't until 1949 that any Legislative Assembly in the country witnessed the election of its first Aboriginal leader. Frank Arthur Calder earned that title when he was elected to represent the Atlin riding that year. Prior to that accomplishment, he recorded another milestone as the first Aboriginal to "graduate from the Anglican Theological College of the University of British Columbia."

- The flamboyant and outspoken Dr. Charlotte Whitton was the first woman in the country elected as mayor of a major Canadian city. Whitton served as the mayor of Ottawa from 1951 to 1956. She lost the 1956 election, but regained her position in 1960 and served until 1964.

- The first woman to hold a federal cabinet position was Ellen Loucks Fairclough. After the 1957 election she was named Secretary of State for Canada.

- The first Aboriginal elected to the House of Commons was Leonard Marchand. In 1968 he was elected as Liberal Party MP for Kamloops-Cariboo and served in that capacity until 1974.

- The first time that 18-year-olds could vote in Canada was in 1970. Before that time you had to be 21 years or older to vote.

- The first Jewish premier of any province was Dave Barrett. He reigned as BC premier from 1972 to 1975.

- The first woman to serve as speaker for the House of Commons was Jeanne Sauvé. She served from 1980 to 1984. Sauvé was also the first female governor general of Canada, a position she held from 1984 to 1990.

- The first Aboriginal woman elected to the House of Commons was Ethel Blondin-Andrew. In 1988 the Liberal Party candidate was elected for the Western Arctic region and served in that position until 2006.

- Rita Johnston was the first woman to serve as a provincial premier. A member of the Social Credit Party, she served as BC's 29th premier from April 2, 1991, to November 5, 1991.

- Avril Phaedra Douglas Campbell, more commonly known as Kim Campbell, made Canadian history when she became the country's first female prime minister. She was Canada's 19th prime minister and occupied the role from June 25 to November 4, 1993. Campbell was also the first Canadian woman (after

British Prime Minister Margaret Thatcher, only the second woman in the world at that time) to sit with the Group of Eight leaders.

- In 1993, Canadians living outside the country were allowed to vote for the first time.

- All inmates in Canada were first granted the right to vote in "federal elections, by-elections and referendums" in 2002. Until 1995, inmates serving sentences of two years or less were allowed to vote during a federal election. That "right to vote" was extended to all convicts in December 1995. However, the Federal Court of Appeal reversed that decision in October 1999. In 2002, the subject was under appeal, and the Supreme Court of Canada ruled that denying prisoners the right to vote was against the Canadian Charter of Rights and Freedoms.

- The late Diana, Princess of Wales, may have made the cause famous, but it was Canada that was the first country to officially, and on a grand scale, focus on the problem of land mines. Mines Action Canada started out as an ad-hoc committee of concerned citizens in 1994. By December 1997 the group had organized to the point where the Ottawa Treaty, banning the use of anti-personnel mines and working toward the clearing of existing mines, had been written and signed by 122 countries. And on March 1, 1999, the Ottawa Treaty became international law.

- You might not have a roof over your head to call home, but in Canada that's not a voting requirement. In 2000, the homeless were welcomed to the polls for the first time.

- In 2004, Aboriginal people in Canada made political history with the formation of the First Peoples National Party of Canada. The party held its organizational meeting in October of that year. In the summer of 2005, another party representing First Nations' concerns, the Aboriginal Peoples Party of Canada, also started organizing, but because neither party had the number of members required to register officially as a federal party, there was talk of a merger. It isn't clear whether this occurred, and at the time of this writing it appeared neither group was active in any concrete way. However, on December 6, 2005, the First Peoples National Party of Canada became an official federal party.

- In the general election of June 13, 2006, the Green Party of Nova Scotia ran a candidate in all of that province's 52 ridings. This was a first for Green Party history in Canadian politics.

Education

*I acted on the information I have been accumulating since
I was three years old.*

–Pierre Elliott Trudeau (1919–2000), prime minister

ONE OF THE INTRODUCTORY clauses of the BNA Act 1867
includes the phrase "Peace, Order and Good Government." The definition of that phrase can be quite exten-
sive, but simply put, it gave Canadians a direction with
which to grow as a nation. It meant that some concerns,
such as education, were viewed differently than others
because they had an overall impact on the entire country.
Education, as journalist John W. Dafoe later wrote, was
absolutely necessary, especially when it came to the
immigrant population. Without education, the country
would "cease to be a Canadian country in any real sense
of the term."

And so it was that the responsibility for basic education
moved from the family and the church to a public and
provincial responsibility. How education was delivered to
the population continued to evolve—from the one-room,
all-age prairie schoolhouse to grade-segregated class-
rooms to private schools to what it is today: children must
attend school until the age of 16.

Of course, higher learning was handled a little differently. Although the first university was established in the
late 1700s, education after grade school originally offered
few opportunities for women. They were schooled long
enough to become teachers, but studying anything else—
or even taking advanced classes as a teacher—wasn't
encouraged or, in most cases, even possible. But thanks to

the diehard commitment of many prominent women,
such as Emily Stowe and Clara Brett Martin, the status
quo was challenged, and, in time, changes made. Today,
Canada prides itself on spending more public dollars on
education than any other country in the world.

First YMCA in Canada

Francis Grafton and James Clexton of Montréal set up the first Young Men's Christian Association (YMCA) in North America in 1851. The unique organization has its roots in Britain in 1844 after the Industrial Revolution drew young men to city centres in droves. One such man was 23-year-old George Williams, a draper by trade, who realized that there weren't a lot of wholesome, extracurricular activities available in the industrial centres. So on June 6, 1844, he established the first YMCA in London "for the improving of the spiritual condition of young men engaged in the drapery and other trades."

After Grafton and Clexton returned from a trip to England, they, too, were concerned for the welfare of their community and saw the organization as a way to evangelize folks not otherwise affiliated with a church.

Physical recreation and religious discussions were the main activities of YMCAs of the day, but it was enough to attract new members and encourage the establishment of YMCAs in other communities. The Montréal club was once home base to James Naismith, inventor of basketball, as early as 1891. Four years later, in 1895, the club invented another favourite team sport—volleyball.

In 1866, the Canadian YMCA War Services began providing recreational and religious activities, along with care packages for Canadian soldiers—an effort that continued through both World Wars. Four years after the YMCA's inception, an adult education component was added to its calendar, offering workers an opportunity to finish their education with evening classes.

First Woman Admitted to the Bar

Clara Brett Martin came from a family that not only believed in education but also had the means to provide the best opportunities for their children. Despite this background, her path to becoming the first woman to pass the bar wasn't without its difficulties. When Clara graduated from high school in 1890 with High Honours in Mathematics, she decided to study law, something no other woman in the entire British Empire had ever done—but she first had to gain entry to law school. Because women adventurous enough to even audit university classes were frowned on, being officially accepted as a student with the Law Society of Upper Canada was nothing short of a miracle.

When addressing the admissions committee, Martin wrote: "owing to the fact of [her] being a lady [she] is aware that the circumstances of her case are different than those of the ordinary Student-at-Law," and that she was appealing to their "broad spirit of liberality & fairness that characterizes members of the legal profession." Her tactfulness caused debate, but her application was still rejected. That's when she took her cause a step further, obtaining the support of prominent women of her day, as well as the Dominion Woman's Enfranchisement Association, in petitioning the Ontario government to pass a law allowing women to study for the legal profession. On April 13, 1892, the petition was made law, and on June 26, 1893, Martin registered as a "student-at-law with the Benchers of the Law Society."

She didn't have an easy time of it. Along with the heavy course load and time spent articling, Martin was subjected to torment from her fellow male colleagues. But that didn't hold her back. Indeed, it may have been the fuel she needed to rev up her engines for a second go at changing the protocol of the day—to not only achieve the right to work as a barrister (someone who could see clients) but also for admittance to the bar as a solicitor (someone who could represent clients in court).

On April 16, 1895, legislation permitting women to be called to the bar was passed in a vote of 61 to 27. Of course, the passing of the bill didn't automatically mean Martin was successful in her quest to work as a barrister and solicitor. When she applied to the bar in the spring of 1896, the Law Society balked. But by February 2, 1897, Clara Brett Martin was called to the bar and admitted as a barrister and solicitor.

For the next 25 years Martin built a successful practice largely centred on family law. In 1923 she suffered a heart attack and died. She was only 49, but in her short life she achieved excellence in her career and also paved the way for equality for women in what was then a male-dominated Canada.

Other Education Firsts

- From 1534, when Jacques Cartier first discovered this country and named it New France, and for many years thereafter, it was the church's responsibility to run and administer the daily duties of schools and education. That changed in the early part of the 19th century when the colonial government first proposed the providing of publicly funded education. That, too, posed problems because religion was an integral part of the schooling of the day, and Protestants and Catholics couldn't agree on how religious education would be delivered. Their solution was to establish two school divisions in both Upper and Lower Canada.

- Canada's first English university is the University of New Brunswick. It was established in 1785.

- In 1663, Monseigneur Francois de Laval, the first bishop of New France, founded a seminary in Québec City, which in 1852 became Universite Laval, Canada's first French university.

- The first organization of any kind to receive the prefix "Royal" to its name is the Royal Institution for the Advancement of Learning. It was granted that honour by King George III in 1801. In 1821 the organization's name was changed to McGill College and bestowed with "Royal Charter from King George IV."

- Queen's University in Kingston, Ontario, was founded on October 16, 1841, and its first classes were held in 1842. In 1858 the institution formed the first student government in Canada—and they were a leader among universities of the day. In 1895, the school's hockey team was the first to challenge for the Stanley Cup. CFRC, their school-run radio station, is the longest running radio station in Canada and the "second longest running radio station in the world."

- The first Provincial Normal School, now known as a teacher's college, opened its doors to students on November 1, 1847. At that time in our country's history, this was the only opportunity for advanced education open to women.

- Dr. Emily Stowe was the first female principal in Upper Canada. Her claim to fame also included her study and practice of medicine (see Chapter Twelve). Initially, Stowe studied at the Provincial Normal School and graduated in 1854 with first-class honours. Following that accomplishment, she was offered a job as principal with the Brantford School Board, a position she held from 1854 to 1856.

- Public education first became the responsibility of the individual provinces with Confederation, in 1867.

- The first woman to graduate with a university degree in the British Empire was Grace Annie Lockhart. She earned her Bachelor of Science degree from Mount Allison University in Sackville, New Brunswick, in 1875.

- The question of literacy and increasing basic education levels in the workplace was first addressed in 1899. Under the tutelage of Reverend Alfred Fitzpatrick, college students spent their summers working in labour camps during the day and tutoring individuals who needed help learning to read, for example, in the evening. From these rudimentary beginnings, Toronto's Frontier College was formed and with it the country's first adult literacy program.

- Calgary's Western Canada High School was originally founded as Western Canada College in 1903 and operated as a private college until 1928. That's when it moved from private to public funding and became Calgary's first composite high school.

- The first junior high school in western Canada was named after Canada's ninth governor general, Albert Henry George Grey. The Winnipeg school opened its doors in 1915.

- First-year students at Newfoundland's Memorial University caught a huge break in 1965. It was the first time that first-year students at any Canadian university were offered free tuition. The provincial government offered and paid for the initiative. Four years later the program was modified, and free tuition was only offered to students based on a "needs assessment basis."

- Although women have attended medical school for more than 100 years, it wasn't until 1999 that a Canadian medical school saw its first female dean of medicine. Dr. Noni MacDonald took over the helm of Dalhousie's Faculty of Medicine on July 1 of that year.

- September 2007 marks the first time that *Maclean's* began to rank Canadian law schools.

The Amazing Canadian Landscape

It is a staggering statistic that half of all the fresh water in the world is to be found in Canada.

–Eric W. Morse (1926–95), writer and naturalist

A BOOK ON CANADIAN firsts wouldn't be complete without looking at some of Canada's amazing geography and reflecting on those people who first traversed it. Who was the first to climb Canada's highest mountain? Who first set eyes on Canada's highest waterfall? How did some of our wilderness mysteries, such as the Sasquatch, come about? Who was the first woman to climb all 54 of the 3350-metre peaks in the Canadian Rockies?

And what about our wetlands? Where are our largest lakes and longest rivers, our smallest and shortest ones? Which Canadians first discovered these watery treasures? How many swimmers have challenged the length and breadth of Canada's large lakes, and who were the ones to emerge victorious? Which European explorers first maneuvered along this nation's intricate system of waterways?

Although what follows is only a brief overview of the Canadian landscape, it does attempt to address some of these questions. The answers offer a different look at Canadian history—a view where human geography intimately interacts with our country's physical geography and, in the process, defines a little bit about what it means to be Canadian.

Mountainous Firsts

To say Canada's many mountains are majestic is an understatement. The Canadian Rockies tower over the Prairies undulating to the east and overlook the smaller mountains to the west. At an amazing 5959 metres, Yukon's Mt. Logan is the second tallest mountain in all of North America, second only to Alaska's 6193.6-metre-tall Mt. McKinley. But it isn't our country's only natural highpoint.

Here are Canada's top 10 peaks, according to Statistics Canada:

	MOUNTAIN	HEIGHT (IN METRES)
1.	Mt. Logan, Yukon	5959
2.	Mt. St. Elias, Yukon	5489
3.	Mt. Lucania, Yukon	5226
4.	King Peak, Yukon	5173
5.	Mt. Steele, Yukon	5067
6.	Mt. Wood, Yukon	4838
7.	Mt. Vancouver, Alaska/Yukon	4785
8.	Mt. Fairweather, Yukon/BC	4663
9.	Mt. Macaulay, Yukon	4663
10.	Mt. Slaggard, Yukon	4663

Anyone who's travelled Canada's Rocky Mountain wilderness areas has got to be asking, "What about British Columbia's Mount Robson?" Well, at a height of 3959 metres, it does hold the distinction of the highest point in the Canadian Rockies. Here are more provincial and territorial high points, according to *The Atlas of Canada*:

PROVINCE / TERRITORY	MOUNTAIN OR HIGH POINT	HEIGHT (IN METRES)
Newfoundland and Labrador	Mt. Caubvick	1652
Nova Scotia	White Hill	532
Prince Edward Island	(unnamed)	142
New Brunswick	Mt. Carleton	817
Québec	Mont D'Iberville	1652
Ontario	Ishpantia Ridge	693
Manitoba	Baldy Mountain	832
Saskatchewan	Cypress Hills	1392
Alberta	Mt. Columbia	3747
British Columbia	Mt. Robson	3959
Vancouver Island	Elkhorn Mountain	2210
Queen Charlotte Islands	Mt. Moresby	1143
Yukon	Mt. Logan	5959
Northwest Territories	(unnamed peak)	2773
Nunavut	(unnamed peak)	693

Momentous Mountain Firsts

- The first European to visit the Canadian Rockies was Anthony Henday in 1745.

- The first officially recorded finding of Sasquatch footprints took place in the mysterious Canadian Rockies in 1811. On January 7 of that year, renowned explorer David Thompson recorded seeing tracks of a large animal during his search for the mouth of the Columbia River. The footprint he found appeared to indicate four large toes, each about three inches (7.62 centimetres) long and tipped with a small nail. He recorded that the ball of the foot sank about three inches into the ground, but the heel of the unknown creature's foot was not as well marked. It measured about 14 inches long (35 centimetres) and 8 inches (20 centimetres) wide, making it the largest footprint he'd ever seen. That same year, another traveller reported actually seeing the hairy giant near Jasper, Alberta.

- The first successful climb of any of Canada's Rocky Mountain peaks was recorded in 1827 after David Douglas, a botanist from Glasgow, Scotland, scaled Mt. Brown, which measures 2791 metres. He came across the mountain while travelling through the Athabasca Pass and named the mountain after his professor, R. Brown, Esquire. Douglas also climbed another mountain, Mt. Hooker, which he named after Sir William Hooker, a fellow botanist with the University of Glasgow.

- The first person in Canada to climb a mountain higher than 3040 metres was James Joseph McArthur. A surveyor with the Dominion Land Survey on a mission to record measurements and photograph the area, McArthur scaled Mt. Stephen on September 9, 1887. He was also the first to climb Mt. Odaray (in 1887), Mt. Rundle (1888), Mt. Aylmer (1889), Mt. Bourgeau (1890),

Mt. Owen and Mt. Burgess (1892). These accomplishments gave him the recognition of being the country's "first true mountaineer."

- The Rockies, despite a challenging reputation, drew visitors and settlers from the earliest days, and people travelling through the region needed a place to stay. In 1886, Mount Stephen House at Field, BC, was the first hotel anywhere in the Canadian Rockies to welcome guests.

- The first group to conquer Mt. Robson included Alberta MacCarthy, William Foster and an Austrian climbing guide named Conrad Kain. They successfully made it to the highest peak in 1913. Because of the snow, ice, risk of avalanches and challenging weather, Kain described the ascent as one of the most dangerous of his career.

- Canada's highest waterfall, surprisingly, is not in the Rockies, but in Strathcona Provincial Park, Vancouver Island. Della Falls is 440 metres high. The first white man to set eyes on the amazing site was Joe Drinkwater in 1899. Likely thinking it one of the most beautiful things he'd ever seen, second only to his wife Della, of course, he named the falls after her.

- The first Canadian mountaineer to tackle the heights of Mt. Everest was Major Edward Wheeler in 1921.

- In 1923, motorists were given more opportunities to travel through the Canadian Rockies when the road between Banff and Radium officially opened. It was considered a major link in "the first public highway" in the area.

- The Canadian Pacific Railway slammed in its last spike in the Columbia Mountains on November 7, 1885, making history as the site where the country's first railway was complete.

- Just outside the Rocky Mountain range, nestled in the northwestern portion of BC, near the city of Terrace, is the Tseax River Cone—a cinder cone that is one of

160 volcanoes that make up the Pacific Ring of Fire. Although the volcano is currently silent, poisonous smoke and gases from its last eruption sometime around 1730 killed as many as 2000 Nisga'a people and completely destroyed two of their villages, making it one of the country's "worst known geophysical disasters." The 22.5-kilometre-long stretch of lava-covered forest is known as the Nisga'a Memorial Lava Beds Provincial Park.

- Newfoundland and Labrador's Mt. Caubvick is considered the highest peak east of the Canadian Rocky Mountains. Two Americans, Christopher Goetze and Michael Adler, first attempted to scale the massive giant in 1973. They successfully scaled the 1585-metre mountain from the east and onto Minaret Ridge. The first people to climb Mt. Caubvick by way of Minaret Ridge were Robert Rogerson, Hazen Russell and Tim Kelliher. The men, all from St. John's, Newfoundland, were part of a research team studying the Minaret Glacier. On July 28, 1982, the three men climbed the Minaret Ridge, and the next day, Russell and Kelliher performed the first ascent of the north ridge. They initially called it "Rogerson Ridge," after their absent partner who decided not to climb that day, but the name was eventually changed to Newfoundland Ridge.

- Jack Bennett and other members of his group completed the first successful climb of Mt. Caubvick's west ridge on August 14, 1997. A year later he was hailed as the first person to climb the highest point in each of Canada's provinces and territories.

- In 2003, Nancy Hansen became the first (and only woman to date) to successfully climb "all 54 peaks over 11,000 feet [3350 metres] in the Canadian Rockies."

Land of Lakes

Although it's not clear how many lakes there are in Canada, as sources differ on the exact figure, some researchers suggest there are as many as three million. Of course, that number most likely includes all the itsy-bitsy lakes that some might call sloughs. However, you only have to look at a map of Manitoba or Ontario to know lakes take up a pretty large portion of the landscape. Here's a list of the 10 largest lakes entirely located inside the country, according to Statistics Canada:

NAME OF LAKE	AREA (km^2)
Great Bear Lake, Northwest Territories	31,328
Great Slave Lake, Northwest Territories	28,568
Lake Winnipeg, Manitoba	24,387
Lake Athabasca, Saskatchewan	7935
Reindeer Lake, Saskatchewan	6650
Smallwood Reservoir, Newfoundland and Labrador	6527
Nettilling Lake, Nunavut	5542
Lake Winnipegosis, Manitoba	5374
Lake Nipigon, Ontario	4848
Lake Manitoba, Manitoba	4624

It's obvious the above list is missing any reference to the Great Lakes, which obviously received that name because of their large size. The omission is because the lakes share a portion of their waterway with the United States. Still, a reference to Canada's large lakes would be incomplete without pointing out just how big these lakes are, according to *The Atlas of Canada:*

Name of Lake	Area (km²)
Lake Huron	59,600
Lake Superior	82,100
Lake Erie	25,700
Lake Ontario	18,960

Of course, every province and territory is proud of its mighty lakes. Here's a list of the biggest each has to offer, according to *The Atlas of Canada*:

Province / Territory	Largest Lake	Area (km²)
Newfoundland and Labrador	Smallwood Reservoir	6527
Nova Scotia	Bras d'Or Lake	1099
New Brunswick	Grand Lake	174
Québec	Lac Mistassini	2335
Ontario	Lake Nipigon	4848
Manitoba	Lake Winnipeg	24387
Saskatchewan	Lake Athabasca	7935
Alberta	Lake Clair	1436
British Columbia	Williston Lake	1761
Yukon	Kluane Lake	409
Northwest Territories	Great Bear Lake	31328
Nunavut	Nettilling Lake	5542

You'll notice that Prince Edward Island doesn't have a "largest lake." That's because it doesn't have any lakes at all, making it the only province in the country with that distinction.

Lakeside Trivia

- The Great Lakes are collectively considered to be the most important inland waterway in the entire world.

- Manitoulin Island, located on Lake Huron, Ontario, is home to the world's largest lake on an island.

- Native people were the first to inhabit the area surrounding the Great Lakes many thousands of years before the first European settlers ventured onto Canadian soil. Some estimates suggest more than 120 different tribes lived in various parts of the northern and southern shores of these lakes, among them were the Chippewa, Cree, Mohawk, Ottawa, Huron, Potawatomi, Onondaga, Sioux and Nipissing tribes.

- The first European expedition into the Great Lakes area was led by Samuel de Champlain in 1615.

- Jim Dreyer, of Grand Rapids, Michigan, is the first person to swim across all five of the Great Lakes, shattering swim records along the way. Among his many momentous moments (all accomplished with the sole goal of raising money for Big Brothers and Big Sisters) was in making a new distance record swim for Lake Superior. In 2005, he covered 77 of his 117-kilometre quest in 37 hours and 38 minutes.

- In 1962, Ontario's Bob Weir swam the 28 kilometres across Lake Winnipeg in a mere 9 hours and 57 minutes. A year later, he became the first person to swim across the much larger Lake Manitoba. It took him 25 hours and 10 minutes to cover the 34-mile stretch.

- The first movie to be filmed along the shores of Lake Winnipeg, and specifically in Gimli, was a 1917 production called *The Wild Goose Chase*.

Longest Rivers

Along with Canada's three million lakes, the country boasts about 755,000 square kilometres of rivers and streams. In the early days of this country, when the land was thick with vegetation and difficult to traverse, rivers and lakes offered European explorers the most effective form of travel. Here's a list of Canada's 10 longest rivers, according to Statistics Canada:

- Canada's longest river is the Mackenzie River. It stretches through the Northwest Territories and through Alberta and British Columbia, for a staggering 4241 kilometres. The only river in North America longer than the Mackenzie is the Mississippi River, and it's the fifth longest river in the world at 3734 kilometres.

- Second longest and almost as impressive is the Yukon River, which flows for 3185 kilometres, though most of that river courses through Alaska.

- The mighty St. Lawrence River ranks third at 3058 kilometres long.

- In fourth spot is the Nelson River, which flows along for about 2575 kilometres.

- At a length of 2000 kilometres, the Columbia River is the country's fifth longest river.

- The Saskatchewan River covers 1939 kilometres.

- The Peace River, which is just slightly shorter than the Saskatchewan River, comes in at the sixth spot covering 1923 kilometres.

- The Churchill River flows for 1609 kilometres.

- The South Saskatchewan is 1392 kilometres long.

- And finishing off the top 10 is the Nelson, which flows for 1370 kilometres.

River Trivia

- The first oil exploration by geologists of the lower Mackenzie River took place in the early 1900s, after the Dene led an expedition to the area. Imperial Oil drilled the first well in the region in 1919.

- On the north bank of the Churchill River stands the oldest building in Saskatchewan. The Stanley Mission's Holy Trinity Anglican Church was built sometime around 1854 and is still in use.

- Jacques Cartier made history when he became the first European explorer to discover the St. Lawrence River. He is also credited with the discovery of the Cabot Strait, located between Cape Breton and Newfoundland.

- The Cree were the first to establish the fur trade in the Peace River region in 1718.

- The first white explorers into the Peace River region were fur traders working for the Hudson's Bay Company (HBC). They arrived in the area in the 1700s, but the first official settlement didn't begin to take root until 1906 after the railway reached the area.

- English explorer Thomas Button first discovered the Nelson River in 1612. The first trading post was established there in 1670 by the HBC.

- Henry Kelsey, another member of the HBC, is the first non-Native man to discover the Saskatchewan River, arriving there in 1691.

- Samuel Hearne established Cumberland House, the HBC's first inland fort, in 1774.

- The shortest river in Canada is Powell River, located in BC. At a mere 500 metres in length, it's also considered the second shortest river in the world; the shortest is Roe River in Montana, which is 61 metres long.

The Environment

Canada, which supplies almost all the world's newsprint, cuts down 247,000 acres per year more trees than it replants.

–Marjorie Lamb, writer, in 1990

IF YOU'VE TRAVELLED through the Rocky Mountains on a fairly regular basis over the last 20 or so years, you may have noticed that the mountains look a little different. Maybe you can't quite put your finger on it, but if you venture as far as the Columbia Ice Fields, it will likely hit you—there's a lot less ice than there used to be, and yes, the mountains have a lot less year-round snow pack, too. Canada's climate is changing, and even with its bold attempt at trying to meet the goals under the Koyoto Protocol, the country—and the rest of the world—is struggling.

Still, our nation takes environmental concerns seriously. Getting to know our land through research has always been something the provincial and federal governments supported. Protecting the environment has also been of equal importance. Canada set up the first bird sanctuary on the entire continent. Banff, the site of the country's first national park, was established in 1885, even before Alberta was a province, and, to date, another 40 national parks or park reserves have been established in Canada. And when Canadians don't think the government is involved enough in environmental issues, they've traditionally rallied together to lobby for change—just ask the folks down at Greenpeace.

First Marine Protected Area

About 250 kilometres southwest of Vancouver Island, roughly 2250 metres under water, is the little-known Endeavour Hydrothermal Vents Marine Protected Area. On March 7, 2003, the Honourable Robert G. Thibault, Minister of Fisheries and Oceans, made Canadian history by naming the area the first marine protected area. Hydrothermal vents (basically geysers similar to Yellowstone's "Old Faithful," only on the ocean floor) spew water as hot as 300°C, and during the process deposit sulphide particles creating sculptures not unlike those found in sulphur caves on land. Hydrothermal vents are a fairly new discovery; the first such vent was found in 1977 near the Galapagos Islands. And while you might think nothing could actually live in these conditions, you'd be surprised to learn there are as many as a half a million animals per square metre in certain locations. At least 60 different species were identified along the Juan de Fuca Ridge, many of them never before discovered, and 12 species aren't known to exist anywhere else. The area has drawn scientists from Canada and around the world to study its unique characteristics since its discovery in 1982.

Other marine areas being considered for protected status include a place called the "Gully." Located about 200 kilometres deep within the Atlantic Ocean off the coast of Nova Scotia, the Gully is thought to be "one of the deepest submarine canyons in western North Atlantic."

First Bird Sanctuary

Greatness sometimes goes unrecognized. Thankfully, Jack Miner, despite being considered a poor candidate for school at age five, went on to do great things for the environment. In 1878, 13-year-old Jack and his family moved from Dover Center, Ohio, to Kingsville, Ontario, and he immediately took to the wilderness surrounding his new home, trapping and hunting to help provide for the family. In 1904, at the age of 39, he founded the Jack Miner Bird Sanctuary—a conservation area set aside for the study and management of Canada geese and other waterfowl—the first bird sanctuary to be established in North America.

He banded his first bird, a Mallard duck, in August 1909, and attached his name and address on the aluminum fastened to the bird's leg. The following year the tag was returned to him with the information that the bird was shot by a Dr. W. Bray of Anderson, South Carolina, on January 14. Miner's simple act completed the first banding record in the entire continent—and it propelled the man once dubbed as unsuitable for school into a lecturing career that spanned three decades.

The first book written about the man and his efforts was entitled *Jack Miner & the Birds* and was published in 1923. By then he'd tagged more than 50,000 birds. In 1929 he was the first Canadian to receive the Outdoor Life Gold Medal, given out to an individual whose work shows "the greatest achievement in wildlife conservation on the continent." That accolade was followed by many more, including the Order of the British Empire by King George VI "for the greatest achievement in conservation in the British Empire."

Although Miner was functionally illiterate until the age of 33 and never received a formal education, his love for waterfowl and his dedication to ensuring their study and conservation was enough to equip him for his life's work. Lovingly known by many as "Wild Goose Jack," he was also frequently honoured with another moniker—"father of North American conservationism." Having tagged more than 50,000 wild ducks and 40,000 Canadian geese during his lifetime, it's a recognition he certainly earned.

Jack Miner died on November 3, 1944. He had dedicated his life to conservation, and his efforts influenced conservation laws across the continent. After his death, his work was further remembered when in 1947 the Canadian government declared the country's annual National Wildlife Week be held every year during the week of Miner's birth. As the *Windsor Star* wrote in 1993, "The week of April 10th was designated as National Wildlife Week to permanently remind Canadians of a pioneer who changed the attitudes of a continent, against great odds."

Greenpeace

Canadians might be a meek, self-deprecating bunch in a lot of ways, but when we really believe in something, there's no stopping us. Greenpeace, the first environmental protection organization of its kind in Canada, is a prime example. Although the group is now international in its scope, with a head office in Amsterdam, it started out simply enough. American expatriates Jim and Marie Bohlen and their friends Paul Cote and Irving and Dorothy Stowe were propelled into action when they heard about a proposed underground nuclear test by the U.S. government near Alaska. The testing was set for Amchitka, which was smack in the middle of a wildlife reserve in the Aleutian Islands. It was also the site of a major fault and long considered one of the world's most earthquake-prone regions.

Rallying friends and family members together and drumming up as much public support as they could, the small group managed to lead a demonstration 10,000 strong with people wielding placards along the Canada–U.S. border, cautioning "Don't Make a Wave. It's Your Fault if Our Fault Goes." The 1969 demonstration received collective support on both sides of the border. But when organizers led a sailing trip right to the site of the proposed bombing in 1971, they lost the support of the Sierra Club in the U.S., a group that they were affiliated with through membership in a Canadian chapter of the Sierra Club in Vancouver. That's when they organized themselves independently under the name "Don't Make a Wave Committee."

The demonstration did its job, at least when it came to raising support for the cause, but it was only a beginning. The cause was gaining momentum. People were genuinely concerned about the effects of nuclear testing on the environment and on the world's human inhabitants, and while it was some time before the group acquired the financial stability to carry out its global protests, clearly this band of concerned citizens weren't going to step back.

The group officially changed its name to Greenpeace Foundation on May 4, 1972. By then they had already conducted several protests that made a difference. Although one hydrogen bomb was detonated in Amchitka on November 6, 1971, public outcry resulting from Greenpeace's efforts had a hand in the U.S. cancelling a second planned test. In 1972 and 1973 the group took action against the French government's plans to test nuclear weapons in the South Pacific. Altercations between the government and the group were far from peaceful, and in the end Greenpeace received financial compensation for damage done to their yacht. More importantly, their efforts resulted in the French government moving their testing to a safer, underground location.

Greenpeace even tackled the use of dangerous chemicals by Apple computers, which resulted in the company discontinuing their use. Wherever there is an environmental concern on this planet, be assured Greenpeace is watching and planning a course of action.

Whoever said Canadians were timid?

Other Environmental Firsts

- The Shubenacadie Provincial Wildlife Park in Nova Scotia established the country's first breeding program for the Atlantic brant, ring-necked and American eider ducks. The park is also home to Shubenacadie Sam. He is Canada's first groundhog to make the traditional February 2 Ground Hog Day prediction on whether spring is just around the corner or whether we'll have another six weeks of winter.

- The first forest research station was established in Ontario in 1918. Called "A Living Laboratory," the 10,000-hectare patch of land near Petawawa is still used as a research forest to this day.

- In the late 1960s, Richard Sewell created Canada's first homemade device to salvage oil from oil spills on waterways—the Slicklicker. The chemist, employed at the time with the Department of National Defence in Ottawa, reasoned that like attracts like, and that if oil repels water, oil would attract oil. Sewell's machine can reclaim as much as 162,755 litres of oil from a spill in a single day.

- The first patch of land the federal government ever recognized as a national park is nestled in the Rocky Mountains bordering Alberta and British Columbia. Banff National Park received this distinction in 1885, just two years after railway workers stumbled across the area's infamous hot springs. The park is also named a UNESCO World Heritage Site.

- The deepest lake in the Canadian Rockies is Upper Waterton Lake, located in Waterton National Park. From there the mountains stretch into Montana's Glacier National Park, and in 1932 the two parks were the first in the world to come together to form the Waterton-Glacier International Peace Park.

- Canada leads the world in maple syrup production, with almost 80 percent of the product coming from this country. About 90 percent of our nationwide collection of the sweet treat comes from the province of Québec.

- The Bald Eagle may be the official bird of the United States, but the highest concentration of the species was recorded north of the border in Canada. In 2001, an official eagle count logged 1942 mature birds and their offspring in Squamish, BC, slightly more than the annual average of 1700.

- Winnipeg's Dr. Elaine Thompson didn't like the way refuse tires were piling up in landfills across the country. So in 1982 she was the first to figure out a way to recycle them into asphalt emulsion, which is then used as a seal coat for roads.

- The highest tides in the world are recorded at the Bay of Fundy. It appears it's all about how the sun and moon line up in the region, because scientists credit these gravitational forces for the tidal extremes that can rise 16 metres at times.

- Leaf Rapids, a northern Manitoba mining town, was incorporated in 1969, but the first permanent residents didn't arrive until 1971. Conscious of how their main industry and economic lifeline would impact the environment, the townspeople took great pains to protect their natural surroundings. The town was constructed with every effort to minimize its ecological footprint while at the same time providing residents with everything required for modern living. Leaf Rapids was the first town in the country to build exclusively with these factors in mind, and in 1975 it was awarded the Vincent Massey Award for Urban Excellence. In March 2007 the town recorded another amazing first, especially when considering the current commercial climate.

Town administrators banned the use of plastic shopping bags by community retailers. The law was enacted on April 2.

- The Geological Survey of Canada (GSC) was formed on April 14, 1842. It was the first agency of its kind in the country to conduct "forestry research and collect specimens for its museum as part of its exploration of Canada's geology." In 1863, the GSC produced the first-ever compendium outlining the land of Canada.

- Native people first began trading in copper more than 6000 years ago.

- The first Europeans to mine for Canada's rich minerals were the Vikings, who, in 998 AD, landed on the shores of Newfoundland.

- The first recorded non-Native discovery of iron and silver in Canada took place in St. Mary's Bay, Nova Scotia, in 1604. According to the Chronological Record of Canadian Mining Events from 1604 to 1943, copper was also discovered that year at Cap d'Or.

- The Forges du St. Maurice, in Trois-Rivieres, Québec, was the country's first iron smelter. It started operations in 1729.

- Canada's first diamond mine was discovered about 350 kilometres northeast of Yellowknife, Northwest Territories. The Ekati Diamond Mine first went into production in 1998.

- Gold was first discovered in 1823 in the province of Québec.

Household Innovations

In science the credit goes to the man who convinces the world, not to the man to whom the idea first occurred.

–Sir William Osler (1849–1919) Canadian physician

CANADIANS ARE NOTHING if not inventive. Give us a chore to do, and we'll discover the most efficient way of carrying it out. Of course, our contribution to such things as the zipper and the screwdriver often go unrecognized or have been forgotten, but trust me when I tell you Canadians have done their fair share of making everyday activities a whole lot easier.

In the 1940s, Canadians designed a portable refrigeration unit to keep foods cool on the war front and help feed British soldiers. It was also a Canadian who invented the paint roller—thank goodness. Another Canadian invented the king of all bug dope, Muskol. And it was a Canadian who came up with the idea that a pop-up handle would make it easier to carry a case of beer.

To ensure Canadian innovation garners the attention it deserves, the Canadian Innovation Centre has been helping inventors and organizations develop their products for about 30 years now. Since it set up first as the University of Waterloo's Inventor's Assistance Program in 1976, and then as the Canadian Innovation Centre in 1981, more than 70,000 inventors have had their ideas scrutinized. Of those, more than "13,000 new product ideas have been assessed," and thousand of others have successfully been guided through the marketing process.

The Robertson Screwdriver

Sometimes the products available to us already serve their purpose. But as anyone knows, there's always room for improvement. Such was the case for Peter Lymburner Robertson, the first person in Canada to invent a new type of screwdriver. The young man, not yet in his 30s, was demonstrating to someone the best way to use a spring-loaded screwdriver, most of which were originally designed to clasp around the outside of a screw head. During his demonstration, the screwdriver slipped off the screw head, giving him a nasty gash in the hand. It was altogether too easy for the screwdriver to slip, and he had an idea of how to correct the problem. Why not develop a screw with a square recessed into the head? By sinking a screwdriver into the screw head, it would be less likely to slip off and cause a cut as he'd experienced.

On August 29, 1908, Robertson advertised his new square-topped screw in a London, Ontario newspaper, calling it the "greatest of all the improvements made in screws—THE RECESSED HEAD." The square hole also had an inverted pyramid tip, providing the appropriate screwdriver with more slip resistance. Of course, that appropriate screwdriver was also something Robertson invented, and on February 2, 1909, he received the patent for his screw, and his P.L. Robertson Manufacturing Company Limited in Milton, Ontario, was well into production.

Developing a machine to economically produce his newly designed screws was yet another challenge—one Robertson met head on. It took another two and a half years before he was satisfied with the machine he'd designed to punch the screw heads with the appropriately sized inverted pyramid. The machine made production more efficient and cost effective, but Robertson hadn't seen his last hurdle yet. In August 1910, a news article in *Saturday Night* charged that his patent wasn't worth the paper it was written on, that he had been denied his patent in 1909 and that his screw was basically a rip-off of an earlier idea patented in 1875. The author of the article was wrong—the patent in 1875 was actually a much earlier version of the patent submitted in 1907 but had been rejected. Needless to say, the poor publicity, regardless how inaccurate, caused Robertson great concern, and the newspaper had some serious damage control to do.

Challenges to Robertson's empire didn't end there. Other companies were developing their own unique screws and attempting to discredit Robertson's patent. But he was a determined man and faced each challenge with strength and poise. Even after he sold his business to U.S. interests, the company he founded continued to be one of Milton's major employers.

Development of the Egg Carton

For eons, folks carried eggs from the farmyard to the store and home in nothing more than a basket or pail layered with linens. It wasn't really a problem until fewer families raised their own chickens and relied more on the grocery store. Shipping large quantities of eggs was pretty tough without damaging at least some of the delicate product.

After overhearing an argument between a rancher and a local hotel owner about who should pay for the eggs broken in transport, Joseph Coyle got an idea. The northern BC resident already had a lot of business experience behind him, having established three newspapers. Coyle ran his newspaper business in Aldermere for five years before moving it to nearby Smithers, and during that time he also tinkered with a design for a crate for transporting eggs.

By 1919 he'd fine-tuned his idea, and the machines he'd need to produce the new-fangled crates, and moved to Vancouver to set up production. Initially, United Paper Products contracted him, but after a year with the fledgling company, Coyle moved to Los Angeles to continue production on his own. The move didn't pan out as he would have liked, in view of the heavy costs involved, and in time he transferred his production to Chicago. It was a good move, and the Coyle Safety Egg Carton was soon being produced in the U.S. in New York, Indiana, Pittsburgh, and in Toronto and London, Ontario.

Jolly Jumper Inventor

As any new parent will tell you, lovely as they are, babies are a lot of work. Sure, we now have washing machines instead of scrub boards, along with all sorts of other timesaving devices, but somehow we're busier than ever—and youngsters seem to need more things to keep them interested.

The Jolly Jumper is one device that parents everywhere have thanked their lucky stars for, and the idea came about when a mother of seven thought back to her own childhood living on Minnesota's White Earth Indian Reservation. Olivia Poole recalled how mothers had hung cloth harnesses from tree branches and let their young children bounce. The design not only occupied the youngsters and provided them with good exercise, but it also gave mom a little time to catch up on daily chores.

Poole experimented with whatever household objects she thought might duplicate what she remembered from her youth, and using little more than a broom handle, fabric and a spring, invented the first Jolly Jumper.

When she and her husband Joseph moved to BC in the 1950s, they ironed out all the kinks in their design and came up with a marketable product. By the end of the decade, their North Vancouver factory was making and selling several thousand Jolly Jumpers each month.

Other Firsts in Baby Care

- The "babyTrekker," a front-wearing, five-position baby carrier that supports an infant and is comfortable for the wearer as well, was created by Judy Pattersen of Winnipeg in 1990. She came up with the design after struggling with other models she'd used with her first two children. By the time Pattersen was expecting her third child, she redesigned the baby carriers she'd been using and moulded them into what she called the babyTrekker. Other parents must have been on the same wavelength, because the cottage industry she developed, making babyTrekkers for her friends and family, ballooned into a full-time business requiring its own manufacturing plant. In 1997, Pattersen was awarded Manitoba Home Business Woman of the Year, and Pattersen Infant Products continues to make families happy.

- If you've ever tried giving a fussy baby a replacement soother after you've lost the original, you've likely noticed that soother number two just doesn't cut it, especially if it's an altogether different make. In 1994, a New Brunswick mom named Barbara Michaud came up with a great solution to the problem. She made an elephant-shaped holder that attaches to the baby's crib and functions as a clean and safe container for the soother once baby is asleep. It's called "Keeps Baby Happy," in case you're interested!

First Nosepumps for Cattle

It goes without saying that necessity is the mother of invention. For Jim and Jackie Anderson of Rimbey, Alberta, what they needed was to find a permanent water source for their burgeoning livestock operation. The couple was the first to invent a way for cattle to get their own water with their invention of Frostfree Nosepumps. Jim and Jackie, the second generation to own the family farming operation, had spent a lifetime raising cattle through drought-riddled summers and frigid winters. And although they managed to haul water for their cattle when needed, they believed there was a better, more permanent solution to the problem—and a more cost-effective and ecologically sound option than one that required expensive electricity.

The couple remembered a conversation they had years before with Walter Diehl, another farmer living in the area. Walter supposed that cattle, being a lot brighter than most folks usually gave them credit for, could learn to pump water from a well, which because of its depth, wouldn't freeze up in cold winters or dry out in summers like a dugout would.

The suggestion intrigued the Andersons, so much so that, with Walter's blessing, they fine-tuned his idea. Jim devised a pump that worked on the same principle as an old-fashioned hand pump, with a few minor adjustments. He reconfigured the design so that instead of pumping with an up and down motion, the cattle could pump a specially designed nosepiece in a back and forth motion. The water would then be pumped into a small trough directly below the nosepiece. This gave the thirsty cow almost immediate gratification, and because the trough was small, no water was wasted. In addition, the water wouldn't freeze in winter or dry up in summer.

The Andersons installed their first pump in September 1999. By then, Jim's design included a method for insulation, a cement pad surrounding the unit to prevent groundwater contamination, and a component that prevented unused water from trickling back into the well and causing potential for contamination. The major cost of the project was in the digging of the well, which farmers can do on their own in many cases, and the well kit itself. Depending on the individual farm, the cost could run on average somewhere between $2000 and $3500. But then the farmer is free and clear of the added expenses of electricity and heating, which is a huge plus when you're looking at farms with large properties and many grazing fields.

Interest in the product has been steady since it was first offered to the general public in 2002, making it another prime example of Canadian ingenuity.

Other Household Inventions

- At least three countries and two different inventors were involved in the controversy surrounding the zipper's invention. Sweden could lay claim to the invention because Gideon Sundback, the fellow responsible for patenting a "separable fastener" in 1913, was born there. But technically, because he was a Canadian working in the U.S. at the time, as far as we're concerned, a Canadian was responsible for the invention of the zipper. The Americans, however, argue that one of their own, a man named Whitcomb Judson, invented a zipper-like fastener in 1896. Either way, it was Sundback who acquired a Canadian patent for his "Lightning Fasteners," and they were used on rubber galoshes called Zippers—which is how the zipper got its name.

- Ruth Adams patented the Reverse Cooking Stove in 1855. It was the first of its kind to "have a warming oven that doubled as a kitchen furnace."

- A Calgary woman, whose name has been lost to history, invented the mechanical skirt lifter in the 1890s. The handy little gadget kept skirt-bottoms from dragging through puddles in a country where roads were still under construction.

- In 1908, a person whose name is not known, invented a hat equipped with a water reservoir in its brim so women could always wear fresh flowers. How considerate!

- John Edlund must have been a boy scout. In 1912, the native of Claresholm, Alberta, concerned that folks travelling by ship should be prepared in case they should sink, like the *Titanic* did that year, invented the "Floatation Suitcase." It was basically a suitcase that when opened, doubled as a full-body suit that could keep your head above water for four days!

- Moses Cardin was a thoughtful husband—either that or he wanted his wife to do double duty. In 1922, he rigged a rocking chair that made it possible for the missus, while she was knitting or putting baby to sleep, to churn butter as well!

- In 1940, Norman Breakey of Toronto invented the paint roller, making life a whole lot easier for housepainters everywhere.

- Ever wonder who invented the easy-to-carry case of beer? As it happens, Vancouver resident Steve Pasjack designed the first corrugated carton with a pop-up handle in 1957.

- Mosquitoes are one of those pesky facts of life, but thanks to Charles Coll of Truro, Nova Scotia, we have ammunition. He developed Muskol, a DEET-enhanced mosquito repellent, in 1959.

- Injury prevention workers and police officers have long been telling bicyclists to don a helmet, but even they likely never conceived of a helmet like the one 12-year-old Gina Gallant came up with in 2000. The Prince George youngster devised a "smart" helmet equipped with LED sensors that light up when a helmet is being worn properly. By the time Gina was 16 she'd been recognized with several other inventions and won science awards for her creation of PolyAggreRoad (PAR), a new type of asphalt made from recycled plastic.

Industry

In Canada preserving energy and industry, with sobriety, will overcome all obstacles, and in time will place the very poorest family in a position of substantial comfort that no personal exertions alone could have procured for them elsewhere.

–Catharine Parr Traill (1802–99), Ontario pioneer and writer

ACCORDING TO THE formal definition, an "industrialized" country is one with "developed economies in which the tertiary [service sector] and quaternary sectors of industry [a climate where companies invest and expand] dominate." Simply put, it's a country with opportunities for socioeconomic growth and services to care for its residents. Canadians take care of our own, but we also have a pretty good history of reaching out to others in less-developed countries by providing monetary and volunteer aid.

Ours is also a country rich in natural resources. Despite the Canadian prairies being cleared of trees to make room for field crops, thereby developing a strong agricultural industry, Canada still harvests and sells a great deal of timber. Some of the largest oil and natural gas deposits in the world are located in this country. The construction industry is booming in most Canadian cities, and the manufacturing sector is solid, despite a spike in the Canadian dollar in 2007 that put a little scare into the hearts of automobile workers. And although Jacques Cartier may have coined the phrase "as fake as a Canadian diamond"—after returning to France in 1542 with a shipload of quartz and fool's gold—precious gems and metals are still tucked away beneath the Canadian landscape.

Alberta's First Oil Boom

You don't have to live in Alberta to know that Canada is one of the world's leading oil producers in the world. With 179.9 billion barrels worth of reserves, the nation is second in size only to Saudi Arabia in oil production, according to January 2007 estimates. But a closer look at some of the finer details behind this fact may surprise you.

- Ninety-five percent of Canada's oil is located in Alberta's oil sands, near Fort McMurray. This northern Alberta city beats out Saudi in having the largest, single oil deposit in the world. The three main, neighbouring areas that make up Alberta's large reserve are Cold Lake, Peace River, and the largest of the three, the Athabasca oil sands. The trio covers 48,000 square kilometres or, to give you a visual image, an area the size of New Brunswick. Along with Alberta's deposit, Saskatchewan and offshore Newfoundland also produce oil, though to a far lesser degree. And contrary to popular belief, it is Canada, and not Saudi Arabia, that is the largest supplier of oil to the U.S.

- Native people discovered heavy, sticky petroleum, known as bitumen, long before white settlers ever landed on our fair shores. The substance was originally used for everything from waterproofing canoes to bug repellent.

- Sources differ over who was the first white explorer to discover oil in Canada. Some point to an American trapper named Peter Pond who stumbled upon bitumen deposits as early as 1778 during his hunting expeditions in northern Alberta. However, 10 years later, in 1788, an expedition into northern Alberta by Sir Alexander Mackenzie made the discovery official. He reported finding "bituminous seeps" so deep he could insert a six-metre-long pole "without the least resistance."

- It wasn't until 1893 that exploration into the value of the Athabasca oil sands received federal funding, giving the Geological Survey of Canada the means with which to conduct their investigations.

- The first well was drilled in the Athabasca area in 1894, and it wasn't long before natural gas was hit and reportedly "blew wild for 21 years."

- Impressive as that discovery was, it wasn't the first major find in northern Alberta. That honour goes to the "Old Glory" natural gas field at Bow Island, a well drilled by Eugene Coste in 1909. The first pipelines pumping gas to communities in the immediate area were laid in these gas fields. It took 86 days to lay the 270-kilometres worth of 40-centimetre pipe connecting Calgary to the Bow Island resource. Once installed, natural gas replaced coal gas to heat Calgary homes.

- If Canada's reputation as an oil-producing country wasn't already cemented, a major strike by Imperial Oil at Leduc, Alberta, on February 13, 1947, certainly drove the point home. The company likely breathed a huge sigh of relief when it occurred; it took them 133 tries, and as many dry holes, before the Leduc discovery.

Other Oil, Gas and Mineral Firsts

- The oldest rock in the world, known as Acasta Gneiss, was discovered in the Slave craton in the Northwest Territories. Using radiometric dating, the exposed portion of the outcrop has been dated to more than four billion years ago.

- The first Canadian community to light its streets with coal gas streetlamps was Montréal. The night was lit for the first time in 1836. Toronto wasn't far behind, installing its first coal gas streetlamps in 1841.

- The first oil well in the entire continent was discovered and initially dug by hand by James Miller Williams in 1858, near Oil Springs, Ontario. It was named "Williams No. 1," and today is the site of the Oil Museum of Canada.

- The first discovery of natural gas on Canada's east coast occurred in 1859 in New Brunswick.

- Canada's first gusher erupted on February 19, 1862, at Oil Creek, Ontario. Cooksville, Ontario's Hugh Nixon Shaw drilled 48 metres before he struck oil, and the gusher produced about 3000 barrels per day.

- The world's first oil company to deal with all aspects of the business, from exploration to sales, was created in 1866 by James Miller Williams of Hamilton, Ontario.

- That same year, natural gas was discovered in southwestern Ontario.

- The amazing miracle that was natural gas was all well and good, but it had one serious drawback for users. It stank. Pure and simple. It was because of the smell that folks were reluctant to use it as a fuel source. So in the 1870s, a chemical engineer named Herman Frasch came up with an idea. Using copper oxide powder, he figured out a way of extracting sulphur compounds, which gives natural gas its stink, making a great many people feel safer in the process.

- Imperial Oil was formed from 16 different independent oil companies in Ontario in 1880.

- They may have been drilling for water, but they turned up black gold instead. In 1883, that Canadian Pacific Railway crew was the first to discover oil in southern Alberta in Langevin Siding (now known as Alderson).

- The first time exports of natural gas to the United States were banned was in 1901. Known supplies were getting scarce, and it was another eight years before the discovery of "Old Glory."

- Alberta's Dr. Karl Clark discovered that if you blend tar sand and hot water, the two particles separate, with the oil floating to the top and the sand sinking to the bottom. He patented his separation process in 1929.

- Although Dr. Clark's first process was useful, he soon learned it didn't work the same in all areas because some sands reacted differently. He continued with separation experiments, and in 1931, he reported to the Alberta Research Council a procedure that involved mixing bituminous sand with soda ash and then washing it in a hot water bath. The process recovered almost 100 percent of the bitumen from northern Alberta soils.

- By 1950, coal energy was already passé, and oil became Canada's "largest single source of energy."

- It wasn't until the 1970s that Nova Scotia logged its first oil and natural gas deposits, which were discovered offshore.

- Large oil deposits were discovered at Newfoundland's Hibernia field in 1979.

- Research continued into the study of new ways of separating bitumen from sand, and in the 1980s Dr. Roger Butler succeeded in developing the Steam Assisted Gravity Drainage.

- Coalbed methane, a natural gas derived from coal, was first commercially produced in Alberta in 2002.

- Royal Dutch and Shell Group joined forces to incorporate a Canadian subsidiary, Shell Canada, in 1911. The company was a strong asset to the oil and gas industry, recording a number of its own famous firsts:

  - They started selling oil in one-quart bottles in 1930, making Shell the first major oil company to do so. One quart cost 35 cents—or $1.40 per gallon!

  - Shell Canada is credited with being the first company to strike it big at Jumping Pound, Alberta, in 1944. The company was also involved in the first major discovery in British Columbia 11 years later.

  - In 1901, John Lineham formed the Rocky Mountain Drilling Company and was the first to start drilling for oil in the Waterton Lakes National Park area in 1902. But it wasn't until 1957 that a major discovery in the area was made by Shell Canada, and five years later the first plant to produce sour natural gas in the area opened for business.

  - Isopropyl alcohol, methyl ketone and butyl alcohol are all chemicals produced from petroleum. It was Shell Canada that, in 1953, first developed the technology needed for their production.

  - Shell Canada opened its first self-serve gas station in Vancouver in 1968.

- Searching for ways to protect the environment, Shell Canada developed its own line of unleaded gas with the introduction of "Shell Ultra" in 1970. They were the first Canadian oil company to sell an unleaded product.

- Shell Canada was the first major oil company to add a convenience store to its gas stations with the opening of the Moncton and Calgary locations in 1972.

- In 1984, Shell Canada became the "first refinery in the world to rely solely on synthetic crude oil as a feedstock."

- In 1986, Shell Canada was the first company to add a "combustion-smoothing spark enhancer" to gasolines, and to date is still the only company in the world to do so.

- Shell Canada, in 1998, pulled out the last of its leaded gas pumps, making it the first Canadian oil company to halt the sale of leaded gas.

Forestry Firsts

- One of Canada's first conversationalists was Archibald Stansfeld Belaney. Otherwise known as Grey Owl, he worked on various environmental projects in Riding Mountain and then Prince Albert National Park until his death in 1938.

- Forestry was Elihu Stewart's passion, and he was the first to devise the mandate of forest conservation and propagation in Canada. Under his guidance, reforestation programs were started and "more than 8 million seedlings were planted." Stewart was known as the father of the Dominion Forest Service, which he established in 1899, and later renamed the Canadian Forest Service (CFS). He was 55 years old when, in 1899, he was appointed the Chief Inspector of Timber and Forestry. By then he'd already worked surveying for the Saskatchewan government and served as mayor of Collingwood. And the Dominion Forest Reserve Act, passed by Parliament in 1906, was a direct result of his lobbying efforts encouraging the Canadian government to focus on the "scientific management of forests."

- In 1900 the country's first forestry magazine, *The Canadian Forestry Journal*, was launched by the CFS.

- The first CFS convention was held in Ottawa from January 10 to 12, 1906.

- The first time a week was set aside to recognize Canada's forests and the forestry industry was in 1920. It was called Forest Fire Prevention Week but in 1967 was re-branded National Forest Week.

- According to Statistics Canada, the forestry and logging industry contributed over $5 billion to the country's economy in 2006.

Manufacturing Firsts

- Canada's manufacturing sector started its engines roaring in the 18th century with the establishment of four gristmills in New France.

- In 1833, *Royal William* was "the first ship to cross the Atlantic almost continuously under steam power." St. Mary's Foundry in Montréal built the engines of the *Royal William*. Montréal's Eagle Foundry had built Canada's first steamboat, the *Accommodation,* in 1809.

- The first manufacturers' association was founded in 1871 in Ontario as a way to promote the manufacturing industry. It was named the Ontario Manufacturers Association, but its name was changed to the Canadian Manufacturers' Association in 1877.

- It was in the early 1880s that hydroelectricity was first introduced in Canada, which greatly benefited the manufacturing sector and other industries. Streets in North America were lit electrically for the first time in 1885. The city of Ottawa recorded that historic first.

- Industrial computers were first introduced into the country in 1957.

Fishing Firsts

- An abundance of fish off Canada's Atlantic coastline was what first drew Europeans and Norsemen to this country. The waters near Newfoundland provided catch for Norsemen in the early 1100s and for the British, French, Spanish, Portuguese and Basques from the 1500s to the late 1700s.

- Scientific research into the fishing industry first began in 1898 when the federal government established floating research stations on the Atlantic coast under the Biological Board of Canada. That entity later became the Fisheries Research Board. By the 1920s, it was already clear that haddock stocks had been depleted, and Canada and the U.S. started to push for conservation.

- The first meeting of the fishing nations harvesting along Canada's Atlantic coastline took place in January 1949, under the auspices of the International Convention for the Northwest Atlantic Fisheries (ICNAF). The meeting involved mostly theorizing and suggestion sharing, but in 1970 the ICNAF was finally given the authority to set "Total Allowable Catch" numbers.

Science and Technology

I knew a mathematician who said, "I do not know as much as God. But I know as much as God knew at my age."

–Milton Shulman (1925–) Canadian writer, journalist and critic

FOR THE MOST PART, we're ignorant of our amazing contributions to Canadian society and to civilization the world over. Ask your friends what scientific or technological inventions were Canadian-made and chances are you'll have a few ideas trickle in. They might come up with the telephone and Alexander Graham Bell, and the odd person might even remember Reginald Fessenden. But I'd lay bets that most of your friends wouldn't know the names Henry Woodward or Mathew Evans—it was they, and NOT Thomas Edison, who invented the light bulb.

According to the website operated by the GCS (Great Canadian Scientists) Research Society, Canada is home to "0.5 percent of the world's population…[but] produces 4.65 percent of the world's scientific publications." Canadian scientists and science discoveries are cited with increasing frequency—"7 percent more than research from the rest of the world." And Canada meets or exceeds the world average in space science and clinical medicine research, and physics.

What follows in this chapter is just a sampling of some of our country's most far-reaching scientific discoveries. And if it occurred to you that the discovery of insulin was a Canadian invention and it's not here, don't fret. An entire chapter of this book is set aside for Canadian medical firsts, and that's where you'll find a story about our medical maverick Sir Frederick Banting.

First Trans-Atlantic Cable

In a world filled with telephones, cell phones, radio-phones, Internet and other countless variations affording options for "reaching out to touch someone," it's easy to take long-distance communication for granted. But did you know that an engineer named Frederic Newton Gisborne of St. John's, Newfoundland, was one of the first Canadians who played a huge role in almost every component of communication technology?

In 1852, Gisborne experimented with insulating wire for the ultimate goal of laying underwater telegraph cables. The idea of long-distance communication had already captured the imaginations of inventors and the general public the world over. In 1825, British inventor William Sturgeon's development of the electromagnet was the first step in producing such technology. Five years later, in 1830, an American named Joseph Henry strengthened the power of the magnet to such a degree that the impulse he sent over a mile of wire was strong enough to ring a bell, thereby establishing what became known as the electric telegraph. In 1835, another American, Samuel Morse, took it from there and created a system that used dots and dashes to send messages over telegraph lines, called Morse Code.

But it wasn't until Gisborne developed a material to protect the telegraph cable wires from natural corrosion from the sea that the idea of communicating across the continent progressed to the next stage. In 1852 he tested his product first in the Canadian waters between Cape Tormentine, New Brunswick, and Carleton Head, Prince Edward Island, and by doing so he laid the first submarine cable in North America. This success gave Gisborne the greater vision of establishing a connection between North America and Europe. The only thing holding him back was money—and a lot of it was needed to produce a cable long enough to travel the 2500 nautical miles between Newfoundland and Ireland, not to mention the cost of installing it.

Gisbrone managed to interest Cyrus W. Field, an American investor, in funding the project in cooperation with Newfoundland's reigning government. Gisborne wasn't involved in a hands-on way, but he—like the rest of the world—was looking on in rapt wonder.

Efforts to lay the cable were made in 1855 and 1856, but both attempts failed. In 1857 the USS *Niagara* was coming up the home stretch laying the last of the line when the cable snapped because of heavy winds. The following year, from July 7 to August 5, 1858, another attempt was made that resulted in a connection between Trinity Bay, Newfoundland, and the most easterly tip of Ireland. The first, trans-Atlantic message, sent on August 15, 1858, from Trinity Bay to Ireland, read:

"Europe and America are united by telegraphy. Glory to God in the Highest, on earth peace, goodwill toward men."

Unfortunately, problems with the insulation severed communications in October of that same year, and it wasn't until July 27, 1866, when another, final and successful attempt was made, this time linking Heart's Content, Newfoundland, to Ireland's shores.

Other Communication Firsts

- The first telegraph cable connecting Canada from coast to coast wasn't completed until January 24, 1885. This feat was accomplished through the Canadian Pacific Railway.

- The final portion of the first cable connecting Vancouver, BC, to Brisbane, Australia, was laid on October 31, 1902.

- The federal government allocated $25 million on February 3, 1960, toward establishing what was then the longest submarine telephone cable of its kind in the world, linking Australia, Guji, and the Hawaiian Islands to Port Alberni on Vancouver Island.

First Telephone Connection

Although sending messages the Morse way, instead of mailing a letter, was a huge factor in speeding up communication, it was missing something. When you read a letter, you feel the warmth of its sender. Dots and dashes spit through sterile wire systems don't have a lot of personality to them. And neither method brings the sender the sound of a familiar voice.

So when Alexander Graham Bell started working on the harmonic telegraph, where tones are produced by electromagnets sending vibrations through steel rods, the basic idea of the telephone began to take shape. If one sound could travel this way, why not the sound of a human voice, which produces its own natural vibrations.

Bell was born on March 3, 1847, in Edinburgh, Scotland, and his family immigrated to Brantford, Ontario, in 1870. A year later he moved again, this time to Boston University to teach visible speech, a concept developed by his father, Professor Alexander Melville Bell, which provided deaf people a means of communication.

By 1874, Bell had joined forces with an electrical worker named Thomas Watson, and for the next year, the pair repeated experiment after experiment, trying to send sound through a wire using only the vibrations of the human voice. Their first success was mediocre at best. Although a sound was finally heard, whatever the sender said couldn't be heard clearly.

The men kept at it, and on March 10, 1876, after two years of painstaking efforts and a prolonged period of time where Alexander Bell was ill and unable to work, they were rewarded for their efforts. The first words spoken, loud and clear over Bell's maze of electrical gadgets and paraphernalia, were, "Come here, Mr. Watson, I want you!"

Bell and Watson were up against another American inventor, Elijah Gray, in the race to register their patent for the project that they had worked on independently. Both Bell and Gray visited the patent office on February 14, 1876, but Bell managed to get there two hours before Gray. To his credit, Gray developed the first electromagnetic receiver. But it was Bell who developed the first workable transmitter.

On August 3 of the same year, Bell clocked another world first, and this time there's no disputing its Canadian origins. He made the first, official telephone call from one building to another when he phoned his uncle David Bell in Brantford, Ontario, from his family's home in Mt. Pleasant, Ontario. Seven days later, Alexander Graham Bell logged the first long-distance call when he phoned Paris, Ontario, from Brantford, 12 kilometres away.

Although Bell was loyal to his Canadian roots and tried to have his invention developed in Canada, he almost lost his patent when George Brown—one of the fathers of Confederation—lost interest in his commitment to establishing the invention in this country. In the end, it was National Bell Telephone from the U.S. that sent a representative to Canada to organize Bell Telephone of Canada.

First Radio Broadcast

By now the world understood the impact of the telephone on the business of life, but why stop at the phone? What if you could transmit the human voice without the need for a hard-wired connection?

Wireless communication is defined as the means of transferring "information over a distance without the use of electrical conductors or wires." It was a concept that captivated the imagination of Canadian-born Reginald Aubrey Fessenden, the first person to transmit a wireless voice message. Reginald was born in Québec in 1866 and showed his academic bent early on in life. At the age of seven he had read *The History of the Decline and Fall of the Roman Empire*, by Edward Gibbons. So it was no surprise that when news of Alexander Graham Bell's telephone experiments flooded local newspapers, the young Reginald was immediately enthralled.

After a stint in a mathematics program at Bishop's College in Lennoxville, Québec, Fessenden accepted a teaching position at the Whitney Institute in Bermuda, and for two years he taught school while fine-tuning his own education, eventually achieving his goal of landing a job with Thomas Edison's laboratory in New York. Fessenden honed his skills during his time with Edison and was employed at several university postings as well as the United States Company, a subsidiary of Westinghouse, all the while working on his pet project. It wasn't until December 23, 1900, that Fessenden transmitted the first wireless voice message from his office on an island in the Potomac River to his colleague who was about one kilometre away: "Is it snowing where you are, Mr. Thiesen? If it is, telegraph back and let me know."

Surprisingly, Fessenden's success wasn't immediately recognized, and Guglielmo Marconi, who received the first trans-Atlantic message in St. John's, Newfoundland, on December 12, 1901, was long thought to be the first to transmit a voice message.

Fessenden made history again on December 24, 1906, when he organized and transmitted the first radio broadcast from his Brant Rock Research Station in Massachusetts. Lonely fishermen and ships' crews dotting the Atlantic coastline were comforted by Handel's "Largo, O Holy Night," and the reading of Luke's Gospel, "Glory to God in the highest and on earth peace, good will to all men."

The first official radio station was actually founded by the Marconi Wireless Telegraph Company of Canada. The station was initially set up in Montréal in November 1918 as a place to conduct experiments, but regular broadcasts began in December 1919.

It wasn't until March 1928 that Fessenden received any concrete acknowledgement of his efforts by way of monetary payment. The Radio Company of America presented him, along with other patent holders whose efforts led to the development of radio, with a cash settlement. Unlike his grandfather before him, an inventor who wasn't recognized for his contributions and died, leaving his family without any financial stability, Reginald didn't die a pauper. When he passed away in 1932, he'd registered more than 500 patents.

First Human and Animal Virology Laboratory

To say the Canadian Centre for Human and Animal Health, located in Winnipeg, Manitoba, is a one-of-a-kind building is an understatement. From all outward appearances, it doesn't look like much. In fact, it looks downright ordinary. But what goes on inside its walls is far from ordinary. No other centre in the world can match some of the claims made here and at Manitoba's National Microbiology Laboratory housed inside.

There are only 15 specialized centres for disease research worldwide like the one in Manitoba. But for several reasons, the Manitoba site is in a class of its own. It contains the country's first-ever Level 4 laboratory, which means it houses and studies some of the world's most dangerous bacteria—such as the Ebola virus and Lassa fever. The lab is also the only facility of its kind in the world to contain Level 3 and Level 4 bacteria, which are the most dangerous strains for both animal and human health. To safely store such dangerous bacteria, everything in the lab is highly processed, from cleaning and re-cleaning the air to sterilizing and re-sterilizing solid and liquid waste materials.

The National Microbiology Laboratory made history in January 2007 when its scientists developed a vaccine against the Ebola virus, which is fatal in 90 percent of cases. Although the vaccine was successful in just four of eight trials, it was hugely significant, because never before had anyone previously exposed to the virus shown improvement following a vaccine.

First in Inventions

While most people have heard of inventors such as Alexander Graham Bell and Reginald Fessenden, the name George J. Klein is a little less familiar. This is a sad fact considering Klein is considered by most of Canada's scientific community to be "the most productive inventor in Canada in the 20th century." Among his many inventions, in the 1940s, Klein led the team that designed Canada's first nuclear reactor, ZEEP.

Born in Hamilton in 1904, Klein spent the better part of his 88 years actively researching and coming up with new ideas, not the least of which was an electric wheelchair for quadriplegics, the microsurgical staple gun, and even an "international system for classifying groundcover snow."

But Klein is especially remembered for his contributions to space and aircraft technology. He spent more than 40 years at the National Research Council of Canada. He also invented the Storable Tubular Extendible Member (STEM) antenna, a high-frequency communication device capable of transmitting signals from space— its use on the *Gemini* and *Apollo* space programs put Canada on the map when it came to space exploration. And although he was retired when Canada was creating another world first with the invention of the Canadarm, he was appointed the project's chief consultant.

Klein died in 1992, and three years later was inducted into the Canadian Science and Engineering Hall of Fame.

Other Science and Technology Firsts

- Let's get a few things straight, shall we. The world has none other than a Canadian inventor to thank for the invention of the light bulb. Sure, American Thomas Edison came along and fine-tuned the handy little gadget, but the groundwork for the idea came along courtesy of Henry Woodward, a medical student from Toronto, and his friend Mathew Evans. The two actually patented the light bulb on July 24, 1874, five years before Edison's U.S. patent. But the young men didn't have the cash to see their project through to the production stage. Along came Edison, who saw the merit of their idea, and he purchased their patent. While Edison saw the project to its completion, the basic mechanics behind the light bulb still use Woodward and Evan's design.

- The "real McCoy" isn't just a saying; it has a history. In 1872, Elijah McCoy was the first to receive a U.S. patent for the invention of a "lubricating cup" that attached to a train's axles and joints and dripped oil. The cup reduced the number of stops a train needed to take in order for workers to manually do the job. (American-born McCoy spent a good portion of his growing years living with his family in Ontario, though he returned to the U.S. and died in Detroit in 1929.) Apparently McCoy's patent didn't stop other wannabe inventors from trying to cash in on their own rendition of the device, but none of them worked as well as the original version, and pretty soon everyone in the railway industry started calling for the "real McCoy."

- Alexander Graham Bell wasn't just a one-hit wonder when it came to his inventive capabilities. During the summer of 1881 he invented the metal detector, which first gained him a little recognition when it was used to seek out a bullet in the body of U.S. President James A. Garfield. It was also considered the "precursor to the x-ray machine."

- Ontario-born John Cunningham McLennan worked as a physics professor for the University of Toronto. In 1915 he was the first to discover how to extract helium from natural gas, greatly affecting its accessibility. He was also a founding member of the National Research Council of Canada.

- The first "working model" of an electron microscope anywhere in North America was developed in the physics lab at the University of Toronto. From 1935 to 1939, Professor Eli Franklin Burton and three students, Cecil Hall, James Hillier and Albert Prebus, worked on the design, which stood 1.8 metres tall. The electron microscope uses electrons to illuminate a specimen and create an enlarged image.

- Getting to know this vast country wasn't easy, and among the challenges new explorers faced was finding a way to map it. The fruits of their labour culminated in the development of Canada's first national atlas, *The Atlas of Canada*, published in 1906. It was only the second national atlas published in the world, the first being Finland. The first French-language version of the atlas was published in 1959.

- Sir William Stephenson was a Canadian hero in both world wars, and some of his undercover exploits are said to have inspired the character of James Bond 007. And on top of that, he was an inventor too. In 1922, after inventing the wireless photograph transmission system, he went on to transmit the first wireless photographs. His work in that arena formed the basis for the development of television.

- You may have heard of the Geographic Information System (GIS)—a system used to store, analyze and manage geographic data—but did you know a Canadian was responsible for inventing the first computerized system of its kind in the world? Roger Tomlinson, often referred to as the "Father of GIS," developed the prototype in 1962. He originally created the system for the Canada Land Inventory to help build a country-wide land database, but from the beginning he was aware of the ongoing potential for his idea.

- It seems as though the planetarium has been around for a long time, but it's actually a fairly new institution. Canada's first planetarium was Edmonton's Queen Elizabeth Planetarium, which opened its doors in 1962.

- On May 27, 1986, Canadian science news hit the *New York Times* after George S.K. Wong, a researcher with the National Research Council of Canada, became the first to amend Charles E. Yeager's theory that the speed of sound was 741.5 miles per hour (331.45 metres per second). While working at calibrating microphones, Wong discovered Yeager's figures were off slightly, and the speed of sound was almost a half a mile per hour slower. Wong's new figures were 741.1 miles per hour (331.29 metres per second).

Architecture

Get over it.

–a popular P.E.I. quote referring to Confederation Bridge

ONE OF THE MOST wonderful things about building a country with as many diverse ethnic influences as those found in Canada is the sheer variety of everything that is produced. The same ethnic diversity that makes the social aspect of life in Canada so rich and interesting also influenced our architecture. Business people moved to Canada and set up shop in buildings not unlike the ones they'd left behind in their home country. The Gooderham Building is an example of this.

French and British styles are strong influences in some of Canada's oldest cities—just visit Basse-Ville in Québec City and you'll see what I mean. And while the unique character and style of some of Canada's oldest buildings has been influenced by the architecture of different countries, Canadian architecture boasts some of its own gems, such as the CN Tower.

Religious buildings, such as Christian cathedrals, Jewish synagogues and Sikh temples, also bring their own unique traditional elements to their architecture.

Canada's First Flatiron Building

With a top floor five stories up, it may not be a sky-scraper, but there's no denying the presence the Gooder-ham Building brings to downtown Toronto. Commonly called the Flatiron Building, the redbrick, three-sided structure was designed by architect David Roberts Jr. and erected in 1891 by British immigrant George Gooder-ham. It was used as headquarters for the Gooderham & Worts distillery until 1952. The flatiron building was the first of its kind to be constructed in a Canadian city, and worth every penny of the $18,000 it cost to build it if you believe those who have toured its interior. Each of the five stories originally boasted 12-foot ceilings, its own vault and, unlike other old buildings that require visitors to use the stairs, contained the first manual Otis elevator ever installed in Toronto. The elevator was refurbished and is still in use.

The Gooderham estate sold the infamous building in 1957. It was designated a historic site in November 1975, and in 1998 it was sold again, this time to Michael and Anne Tippin. Almost as alluring to visitors as the reno-vated building is the mural covering the building's nar-row back wall. Painted by Derek Besant, the mural is like a reflection of the Perkins Building, which is located directly opposite the Gooderham Building.

Other Building Firsts

- Canada's first Anglican church was built in Newfoundland sometime before 1698. The oldest Anglican church still standing is St. Paul's Church in Halifax. It was erected in 1750, became the first Anglican cathedral on the continent in 1787 and, in so doing, became the first British cathedral overseas. It's also the first Protestant church in Canada.

- Most historians consider the first building in Toronto to be the Scadding Cabin. Built by the Queen's York Rangers in 1794, the small, two-storey log cabin was constructed for John Scadding, the executive assistant to John Graves Simcoe, the first lieutenant-governor of Upper Canada.

- The first synagogue in Canada is the Congregation Emanu-el Temple. Construction began on the synagogue, located in Victoria, BC, in 1863.

- Western Canada's first school building took seven months to complete, from August 1854 to February 1855, but the Craigflower Schoolhouse still stands to this day.

- The country's first Indian temple is the Abbotsford Sikh Temple. The 1.5-storey, wood frame structure was erected between 1910 and 1912, and provided a place of worship to Sikh immigrants who were working mostly in the lumber industry at the time. In fact, their presence was so important to the industry that the Abbotsford Lumber Company donated the lumber for the temple's construction. The site has been named a national historic site.

- The first area designated as "Chinatown" in Canada is in Victoria, BC. It started development in 1858.

First, Tallest Freestanding Structure

From its original Huron inhabitants to its first European settlers, the area now called Toronto has always been prime Canadian real estate. The CN Tower in Toronto became the first, tallest freestanding structure on land in Canada and in the world in 1975 before construction was even completed. It held the title for 32 years.

Incorporated on March 6, 1836, the city of Toronto had a population of 9000 back then, which has skyrocketed to today's eight million people, making it the largest city in Canada. As with any kind of growth, there are challenges, and by the 1960s it became increasingly clear that Toronto's many tall buildings were overshadowing the transmission towers, interrupting radio and television signals. This was the impetus for the building of the CN Tower whose primary responsibility was telecommunications.

It took years of planning, 40 months of construction and about $63 million before the CN Tower celebrated its grand opening on October 2, 1976. At a height of 553 metres, it's equivalent to stacking the length of five and a half football fields on top of each other.

CN Tower Fun Facts

- The American Society of Civil Engineers named the tower one of the Seven Wonders of the Modern World in 1995.

- On September 12, 2007, the Burj Dubai—a skyscraper being built in Dubai, United Arab Emirates—succeeded the CN Tower as the world's tallest freestanding building. When it is finished, sometime in 2008, it's expected to be the tallest building in the world by any definition.

- The CN Tower was named after the Canadian National Railway, the company that built the tower. When ownership of the building was transferred from the CNR to the Canada Lands Company, a Crown corporation, the abbreviated name was kept, but it now means Canada's National Tower.

- Although it was built for its broadcasting facilities, the tower is a tourist draw. Every year about two million people visit the building.

- To accommodate all its visitors, the tower boasts a restaurant with seating for 360 people and a café that can seat another 300 people. The restaurant, set at 351 metres, has the distinction of being the "world's highest and largest revolving" eatery.

- If you bypass the elevator in favour of taking the tower's stairs—all 2579 of them—you'll have walked the world's longest metal staircase—and likely dropped a pound or two along the way!

- Lightning season in Toronto usually runs from April to October, and during that time, on average, the tower usually stands up against 75 lightning strikes.

- The CN Tower has a time capsule whose secret contents aren't all that secret. Among the items packed away for posterity are a letter from Prime Minister Pierre Trudeau, copies of each of Toronto's daily newspapers, a sampling of the day's Canadian currency and a video chronicling the tower's construction. The time capsule is scheduled to be opened in 2076 during the tower's 100th birthday celebrations.

First Links Between P.E.I. and Canada's Mainland

Archaeological research into the history of Prince Edward Island suggests Native people inhabited the area as early as 10,000 years ago. Tribes such as the Mi'kmaq lived off the land and surrounding sea, venturing to the mainland only in summer months and, because they were travelling by canoe, only when the weather was extremely calm.

When the French came along in 1720, they were the first group of European settlers to lay claim to some of the island. Although life on the island was soon comfortable and self-sustaining, waiting for the right weather to travel to the mainland to conduct the business of establishing a new government wasn't considered a viable option. The men needed a way to communicate with their superiors across the Atlantic, and their womenfolk wanted to stay in touch with the extended families they'd left behind. In short, the settlers needed a mail service. The problem was how to go about it safely, especially during winter.

At first, using a canoe on open waters and portaging across solid ice flows between the southeastern tip of Prince Edward Island to Pictou, Nova Scotia, was the only option. It wasn't long before the first "ice boat" was designed, giving mail carriers a little more security, but it was still dangerous. Something had to change.

On May 20, 1873, Prince Edward Island was admitted into the Dominion of Canada. One of the provisions included an "efficient steam service for the conveyance of mails and passengers to be established and maintained between the island and the mainland of the Dominion, winter and summer, thus placing the island in continuous communication with the Intercolonial Railway and the railway system of the Dominion." It turned out to be an expensive provision, one that wasn't dealt with permanently for more than 100 years.

For the next 30 years, attempts at meeting the provision fell short of their goal. In 1912, Robert Borden was the first to make headway in establishing a permanent link by instituting the first railcar ferry. As automobiles gained popularity, pretty soon auto decks were added so folks could drive while on the island, but the solution was still far from perfect. What they needed, many thought, was a permanent link between the island and the mainland.

Serious consideration on what kind of link that would be began in 1985 and continued for almost a decade before the people were asked for their official opinion on the matter, and on January 18, 1992, they voted 59.4 percent in favour of going ahead with the building of the Confederation Bridge.

The 12.9-kilometre-long bridge, the first permanent link between mainland Canada and Prince Edward Island, opened its two lanes of traffic in May 1997. It cost a total of $1 billion to complete and remains the world's longest uninterrupted span bridge.

Other Architectural Firsts

- The Hartland Covered Bridge in New Brunswick measures 390.8 metres in length and spans the St. John River. It first opened on July 4, 1901, and is the longest covered bridge in the world. The Hartland Bridge Company built the bridge, but New Brunswick's provincial government purchased and took control of it by 1906. An ice flow on the river knocked out part of the bridge in April 1920 but it was repaired, and the bridge is still used to this day.

- West Edmonton Mall in Edmonton, Alberta, is one of the world's largest indoor shopping malls and amusement centres. Built in four phases, from 1981 to 1998, the entire site covers 154 hectares (or 271 acres, which, if you look at it another way, translates into 5.3 million square feet), and is home to more than 800 retail stores along with assorted restaurants and activities. The mall also contains the world's largest indoor amusement park, Galaxyland Amusement Park, making the mall a Canadian and world first!

Transportation

*A Canadian is someone who knows how to
make love in a canoe.*

–Pierre Berton (1920–2004), writer

I'D BE WILLING TO bet that at least once in your life you've
complained about some of the roads you've driven on.
Either there's too much construction during summer, too
many potholes in spring or it's too darned icy in winter. We
get used to a way of living, so it's easy to forget how great
we really have it. I know I don't go around envisioning
what it must have been like to travel the hour or so between
the prairie community I live in and the nearest city via
horse-drawn carriage over mud paths. Still, while doing
research on this subject, I was surprised at just how interesting something as mundane as transportation could be.

The Prairies are, in places, devoid of anything resem-
bling a tree, but it wasn't always that way. New settlers to
this land often travelled by canoe through Canada's waterways because the thick bush covering this vast country
was almost impenetrable. And even with today's modern
technology, constructing highways through the Rockies
or laying new track for our railway is challenging at best.
Then, of course, there are those innovative vessels and
vehicles built to help humans move a little faster or a little
farther than we could on our own steam—the snowmo-
bile, for example. You can thank a Canadian for that one.

Necessity, and good old-fashioned Canadian ingenuity,
resulted in several "firsts" when it came to devising ways
to travel across this vast country of ours. So read on, and
the next time you hit a pothole, remember, it could have
been much worse.

First Mode of Water Travel

When you're entering another people's territory, it pays to learn by their example. Early settlers to Canada didn't always like that idea. Almost without exception, they envisioned themselves as coming into a land that needed to be civilized—a place where progress hadn't seen the light of day. This was especially true when it came to travelling the country's many rivers and streams—the most sensible way of traversing a thickly wooded wilderness. These explorers watched Native people transport themselves and their goods along sometimes-treacherous stretches of river in flimsy birch bark canoes—they were often heard to comment that the canoe looked like little more than a "dried leaf." But the original inhabitants of this country had accumulated centuries of experience, and the canoe was just one example of their ingenuity. Birch bark was the preferred method of canoe building among the Native people of the Canadian Shield. There, birch trees were plentiful. The men cut down between 8 and 12 trees to make a single, birch bark canoe. In preparation, the women boiled tree roots to use as sinew in sewing the strips of birch bark together. A resin was then used to coat and waterproof the finished structure, making it a lot sturdier than it may have looked to Europeans just stepping off big ships.

But one method of making a canoe didn't necessarily fit all parts of the country. Even back then, birch trees were scarce in western Canada, and Native people living there hollowed entire tree trunks to craft dugout models. And in the northernmost part of the country, whalebone, driftwood and sealskin were the ingredients used in building the kayak.

First Snowshoes

If white settlers in Canada needed to learn a thing or two from the country's original inhabitants, it didn't stop with water travel. How on earth do you trudge through all that snow without sinking hip deep with every step? While some experts suggest the snowshoe was first developed as far back as 6000 years ago in central Asia, Native people most certainly fine-tuned the original rustic version to suit conditions in this country.

Snowshoes are made using a thin strip of wood pliable enough to round at the toe and join at the heel. Deer gut or some other webbing is woven around the wood, forming the bottom of a wide, flat shoe. The large area of webbing provides a wide surface to distribute the wearer's weight, preventing them from sinking.

In 1969, Commissioners Stuart M. Hodgson of the Northwest Territories and James Smith of the Yukon, along with Governor Walter J. Hickel of Alaska, joined forces to establish the Arctic Winter Games committee. The first such games were held the following year in Yellowknife, and while snowshoeing wasn't immediately considered a competitive sport, it was introduced in 1974 and has been a continuous staple in the annual event ever since.

First Toboggans

Of course, getting yourself over the snow is one thing. But how about all the supplies a person needs to get by in life? Native people came up with an answer to that problem as well, with the invention of the "komatik," or what we today refer to as a toboggan. Although wood is used in the mass production of the toboggan, originally the wood bottom was reinforced with bone crossbars. Handles were made with caribou antlers or bone, and if the sled bottom showed signs of wear and tear over time, runners, or "sled shoes," were made from bone or ivory that lined the bottom.

The komatik was adapted for different conditions and terrains and was made from the materials available. Over the years a cariole was developed from the earlier komatik, adding sides and a partial covering overtop. And finally the sled was developed with a view to better handling over ice and frozen snow packs.

Although the toboggan might have been developed for more practical purposes, if you can have a little fun while working, why not? Canada's most northern residents took time out from their many duties to use their sleighs for a makeshift race here and there, and it wasn't long before eastern residents of this vast country caught on to the thrill. In 1881, the country's first official organization dedicated to the new sport—the Montréal Tobogganing Club—opened its doors to members.

First Disposable Ship

No section on transportation would be complete without including a mention of what might be the oddest vessel of all time, the disposable ship. Made completely of squared logs temporarily fit together for the Atlantic crossing from Canada to Britain, this ship was built for one purpose only—to be dismantled once it reached its destination and sold piece by piece. Weird? At first glance you might think so, but it was actually an ingenious plan to provide Britain with a shipment of lumber that wouldn't face the import taxes being imposed during the early 1820s on oak and squared pine.

The sneaky idea was the brainchild of a man we only know as "McPherson." His first disposable ship, which he aptly named *Columbus*, weighed 3690 tons and left Québec City on its journey to Britain via the St. Lawrence River in 1824. And guess what—it arrived in one piece! Everyone was obviously a little too elated with the feat, because instead of dismantling it as planned, the ship's crew turned around and tried to sail back to Québec City. However, as seaworthy as any disposable ship might be, it was no match for a second trip and a deadly storm. The ship and everyone on it perished at sea.

Of course, the point was that the ship made it the first time, and McPherson did what any dedicated entrepreneur would do—he built a second ship. This one weighed almost twice as much as the first, at 5294 tons, and was 95 metres long, making it the largest ship in the world at the time.

To this day McPherson is the only man to build not one but two disposable ships. This time when the vessel arrived in Britain, it was dismantled as planned, and no lives were lost.

First to Drive Across the Country

What started out as a company's publicity stunt has gone down in Canadian history as an amazing first. In 1912, Ransom E. Olds—of the Oldsmobile car company in Michigan—had just finished designing REO the Fifth (so named because it was the fifth such car he'd designed). This version boasted a four-cylinder, 35-horsepower engine, and to make sure the world knew his latest was his best, Ransom provided a sparkling new unit to a man named Thomas Wilby and his sidekick Jack Haney. The two men were supposed to do something no one else had ever done—drive across Canada, from Halifax, Nova Scotia, to Port Alberni, Vancouver Island.

Wilby, a freelance writer, was equipped with the paper and pens required for all the copious notes he'd planned to take for the book he'd later write. The enterprising young man had already completed a 105-day motor trek across the U.S. and was about to begin the Canadian leg of the adventure, which was considerably more challenging. The Trans-Canada highway didn't exist back then; there was little more than a path to get from coast to coast and, directionally speaking, it wasn't exactly as the crow flies.

That's where Jack came in. He would do the driving. As a trained mechanic, he'd also be able to make any necessary repairs to the REO should some of the roads prove a little too rough around the edges. On August 27, 1912, the pair set off, Vancouver bound. They plodded their way across the country, over challenging roads that sometimes forced them to load the car on a ferry (to get across Lake Superior), or on the train (near Lytton, BC, where roads were non-existent). And on at least one occasion travelling over some roads resulted in a twisted drive shaft and a several-day wait for a replacement part. On their best day, they travelled 298 kilometres, which was a considerable feat back then. On their worst day, the men only covered 19 kilometres before they needed to stop and tend to the REO. In the end, despite all their challenges, the men completed their journey in 52 days (or 49, according to some sources).

The trek brought publicity to Ransom Olds and his REO, but it did considerably more than that. In a romantic sort of way, it united a country, so much so that the original 1912 trek was duplicated at least twice, following Thomas and Jack's original itinerary as closely as possible—once in 1960 and again in 1997. The second re-enactment even left Halifax and arrived in Victoria on the exact days of the original journey.

Although the roads were better the second time round, the journey was more than 1000 kilometres longer— 6700 kilometres in the original trek and 7841 kilometres in 1997. And in case you were wondering, it wasn't until 1946 that motorists could finally travel coast to coast without driving at least part of the way on railway tracks.

First Coast-to-Coast Highway

Perhaps it was the success of Thomas Wilby and Jack Haney in 1912 that gave some folks the impression that Canada didn't need a coast-to-coast highway when it was first proposed as early as 1905. But if they had spent any time with Wilby and Haney, they'd have known that was nothing short of ridiculous. Even in December 1948, when federal and provincial officials finally met for the first time to discuss the concept of building the Trans-Canada Highway, some roads linking parts of the company were inaccessible six months of the year.

Although money was being funnelled to the provinces to help build a coast-to-coast highway from 1930 to 1937—$19 million in fact—it wasn't until December 10, 1949, that the federal government finally passed the Trans-Canada Highway Act. The Act guaranteed the federal government would pay part of the cost of constructing the highway—previously the building of roadways was the responsibility of individual municipalities. At that point they committed $300 million to the project, with the idea that the provinces would put up the rest. In the end, the feds paid about 90 percent of the construction costs. Here are a few tidbits on the Trans-Canada Highway:

- Prime Minister John Diefenbaker officially opened the highway with a ceremony at Rogers Pass, the last section of the highway made passable. It was September 3, 1962. Although the highway was completed then, construction continued until 1971.

- The highway is 7821 kilometres long from its farthest point east and west, connecting all 10 provinces and passing through six time zones. However, there are two routes to the Trans-Canada Highway, and with the addition of the 2960 kilometres making up the Yellowhead portion, it measures a total distance of 10,781 kilometres.

- When it was built, it was the world's longest continuous trans-national highway, a distinction some say it continues to maintain. Some sources, however, dispute the claim, giving it a third-place ranking behind the Trans-Siberian Highway and Highway 1 in Australia.

- Victoria has the distinction of being considered "Mile 0." Of course, the folks down in St. John's, Newfoundland, don't agree. They feel that title belongs to them, and they've named their convention centre and sports concept Mile One Centre, just in case anyone disagrees.

- The two most difficult sections of highway to build were the 265 kilometres between Ontario's Lake Superior and Sault Ste. Marie, and the portion joining Revelstoke and Golden, BC, a 147-kilometre stretch known as Rogers Pass.

- If you're on a cross-country trek and reach Batchwana Bay, Ontario, congratulations. You're halfway there.

- At an elevation of 1643 metres, Kicking Horse Pass is the stretch with the highest elevation—316 metres higher than Rogers Pass.

Longest Street in the World

For the most part, Canada was still a babe in the woods in 1793 when the country's first lieutenant-governor of Upper Canada (Ontario) noted a problem. France and Great Britain were at war, and John Graves Simcoe was worried that French supporters in the U.S. might take it upon themselves to try to take over British North America on France's behalf. Plotting a strategy that would put Canada in a stronger position to defend itself, Simcoe established the town of York (now Toronto) in the relatively protected Toronto Bay. The next on his to-do list was establishing an overland route from Ontario's new capital city to the northern Great Lakes. That way, should the Americans invade from the water, access to these areas wouldn't be cut off completely. The new route would also provide fur traders, farmers and other travellers with a main roadway.

Following the trail through the forest already established by the country's Native people, Simcoe's road-building project was underway. The first part of the road, which started out in Toronto and ended at Lake Huron, was completed on February 16, 1796, but construction didn't end there. Work continued on, clearing away the thick Ontario brush, until 1965. That's when it reached the 1896-kilometre mark at Rainy River, a small town near the Manitoba and Ontario border, and Yonge Street officially became the longest street in Canada—and the world.

Length isn't the only thing that makes Yonge Street stand out. Here are a few more amazing facts:

- Catching thoughtless shopkeepers who swept their litter onto Yonge Street was one of the first jobs of Toronto's first police force in 1834.

- Timothy Eaton opened his first store at 178 Yonge Street in 1869, and in the process he set about revolutionizing the shopping industry. The business practices he introduced to Canada were one price for all, no haggling, no credit, money-back-guaranteed merchandise and the mail-order catalogue.

- Public television made its grand debut outside the Eaton's department store in August 1933.

- Long and impressive as it certainly was, paving the way for progress with the construction of Yonge Street didn't answer all the needs of a growing city. By 1945, traffic on the route was so heavy that the city fathers of the day recognized the problem officially, acknowledging that the congestion threatened "the very economic life of our city." After prolonged discussions between political bodies and the public, construction of the country's first subway system was approved on January 1, 1946. Construction began on September 8, 1949, and the first 12-station stretch opened in 1954. Today, the subway covers 68.3 kilometres of track, has 69 stations and is the country's "largest rapid transit rail network."

- If you ever have a hankering to travel the entire length of Yonge Street but don't have your own wheels and think hailing a cabbie is the answer, be prepared. The entire 1896-kilometre trip will cost you no less than $2000.

First Snowmobile

Children are great. They have no concept of the word "can't" and are a lot more apt to take an idea and run with it. Such was the case of a young man named Armand Bombardier of Valcourt, Québec. Much to his parents' dismay, Armand would tinker for long hours in the family's garage, switching up engines and playing with structures and frames in a single-minded quest—to build a snow vehicle that could handle the worst conditions Mother Nature threw at it.

It was just before Christmas 1922 when Armand and his brother Leopold blasted out of the family garage and soared over the snow-encrusted streets of their hometown onboard their newly constructed snow vehicle. Armand was 15 when he just about gave his parents, and indeed anyone in the village that witnessed the spectacle, a heart attack. About one kilometre down the road, the young boys ploughed into the broadside of a barn, thankfully uninjured, but it was enough for their father to make some serious plans for taming that wild Armand of his. Shortly after the incident, Armand registered at a Catholic seminary, and his parents breathed a sigh of relief. At least there he wouldn't kill himself—or anyone else for that matter.

Of course, you can't keep an imaginative spirit like Armand's down for long, and before his parents got too comfortable with the idea of their son becoming a priest, he talked them into letting him explore an apprenticeship with a local mechanic. Armand's drive to tinker and create couldn't be limited to working for someone else, and once he completed his apprenticeship, Armand's father helped him set up his own garage—La Garage Bombardier. Armand still played with the idea of building a vehicle to soar over the snow, but his business was so successful that there weren't enough hours of the day to allow him the privilege of more than a few stolen moments for his pet project.

That changed drastically after his two-year-old son Yvon, stricken with acute appendicitis, died in his arms. The roads were blocked with snow, and he couldn't travel to the hospital where doctors could surely have saved the boy's life. From that moment on, there was no stopping Armand. He fiddled and reconfigured things until some of the problems he'd struggled with were ironed out, and in 1935 he built his first snow-car. In that first year he produced six prototypes, and all six sold—and he, in turn, sold his garage and began concentrating on the snow-car full time.

By June 1937, he had improved the B7 (Bombardier seven-passenger snow-vehicle) and could barely keep up production to meet the demand. He also received his first major patent that month.

During World War II, Armand's largest client was the military. They wanted B7s, but they also wanted the much larger B12s. However, the years following the war reduced the demand. There was no longer a market for these larger snow-machines, so Armand did what any smart businessman would do. He went back to the drawing board and came up with something consumers did want. Eventually Armand created the smaller, one and two passenger Ski-Doo. (It was originally named Ski-Dog, but an advertising typo so intrigued Armand that he kept the name.)

Today, Bombardier Inc. is a multinational company that continues to expand to meet the demand. The company is not only the backbone of the snow-machine industry, but it also creates some of the most advanced fire-fighting aircraft in the world and is the brains behind the Sea-Doo (basically a Ski-Doo on water). And to think it all started with an inquisitive youth.

~⋈~

Other Transportation Firsts

- He may not be as well remembered as the Wright brothers, but Victoria, BC's William Wallace Gibson made aircraft history for this country. An airplane enthusiast, Gibson designed and built a twin-plane and took it to the skies in September 1910, making him the first Canadian to do so.

- Among Alexander Graham Bell's 18 individual patents, and the other 12 he shared with co-inventors, was Canada's first hydrofoil boat. Although other inventors played with the idea of a boat that could skim over the water, Bell and Frederick W. "Casey" Baldwin developed the first successful prototype in 1908 while working on Baddeck Bay, Nova Scotia.

- The first woman in the country to earn a private pilot's licence was Eileen Vollick. She was just 19 years old on March 13, 1928, when she proved to Canadians everywhere that flying wasn't only "a man's sport."

- Frederick Knapp of Prescott, Ontario, set out to build a boat that would roll with the waves, reducing jarring and bouncing and eliminating seasickness. In 1897 he unveiled a long, cylindrical-shaped boat that had another cylindrical-shaped cabin inside that remained stationary while the outer shell rolled along. It was impossible to control, making it one of those inventions that just didn't float.

- The "Norseman" was the first Canadian-designed aircraft specifically built for the cold and rugged conditions of Canada's north. Robert Noorduyn designed the prototype in 1934 and made his first flight out of Montréal in 1935.

Space Exploration

Per aspera ad astra…Through adversity to the stars.

–Julie Payette (1963–), Canadian astronaut

WHO, AS A YOUNGSTER, hasn't stared into the night sky in wonder? We've all, at one time or another, found ourselves mesmerized by shooting stars, a crater-covered moon on a clear summer night or the thick swash of the Milky Way that covers the sky like pixie dust. Anyone alive in July 1969, from the youngest child to the most elderly senior, couldn't help but gasp in awe when a special television broadcast aired film of American astronaut Neil Armstrong making history as the first man to walk on the moon, taking that "one small step for man, one giant leap for mankind." After that, children everywhere dreamed of someday becoming astronauts themselves, blasting off into outer space and maybe even finding life on Mars.

Although space exploration is still in its infancy, a lot has happened since the Russian satellite *Sputnik 1* blasted off into space on October 4, 1957. And while Canada has yet to launch its own fully equipped mission to Mars, it has contributed to the space industry in crucial ways. Canadian scientists have worked hand in hand with the National Aeronautics and Space Administration (NASA), as well as the international space science community. We've not only clocked a few firsts ourselves, such as launching the world's first national domestic satellite with *ANIK A1*, but some of our innovations also have been crucial in providing safer space travel for all nations.

First Contribution
to Space Exploration

The earliest evidence of humankind's obsession with outer space is found in prehistoric cave paintings throughout France and Spain, many of which even focused on the phases of the moon and various constellations. Some have speculated that ancient, standing stone formations, such as Stonehenge, are aligned with the stars. In more recent times, astronomer and mathematician Nicolaus Copernicus is credited with abolishing the theory that Earth was the centre of the universe and, as a result, the starting point of modern astronomy.

Canadians, too, have distinguished themselves as world leaders when it comes to space exploration, launching its first satellite, *Alouette I*, in 1962. Although Canada is a land of promise, its budget for space exploration is limited compared to some countries. So the nation's space program collectively decided to refocus their efforts on specific areas of research. And one of our most notable examples of space exploration greatness is in the development of the Canadarm.

In a nutshell, space exploration is expensive, and it can be dangerous. Problems with an orbiting satellite or other mechanical issues often required maintenance, and designing something that could operate like a human arm would limit the need for human intervention outside the relative safety of the shuttle.

In 1974, after accepting a challenge from NASA, members of the Canada National Aeronautical Establishment of the National Research Council, in conjunction with scientists and engineers from Spar Aerospace Ltd., RCA Canada, CAE Electronics Ltd. and DSMA Atcon, joined forces to design a robotic arm of mammoth proportions and near-human capabilities. The end result of their efforts was the Canadarm, a Shuttle Remote Manipulator System that's built and acts like a human arm. The Canadarm is divided into two parts by a "joint" and is equipped with a pincer at one end that functions as a "hand." The first version was 15 metres long and was threaded with 14 kilometres of wiring. It weighed 480 kilograms, and although it can lift about eight times its weight in outer space because of gravity, it cannot lift its own weight on Earth.

The Canadarm made its debut in 1981 on the U.S. space shuttle *Columbia*, extending into outer space for the first time while hoisting a Canadian flag, and although it was never tested in a space environment, it worked exactly as everyone involved hoped it would. "Seeing the arm deployed without a hitch showed that the eight years of hard work had paid off with a spectacular success," Dr. Garry Lindberg, the first program manager for Canadarm, told CBC National News.

Since then the Canadarm has worked in more than 50 missions "flawlessly." Using a television monitor, astronauts can manipulate the arm to complete all kinds of operations, from putting satellites into orbit to recovering malfunctioning ones.

In May 2001, Canada celebrated another first when the Canadarm2, a newer and even more successful version of the Canadarm, was delivered and assembled on the International Space Station.

Other Space Firsts

- In 1839, the University of Toronto became home to the country's first magnetic observatory. It was established by Sir Edward Sabine to study the earth's magnetic field and its role in the formation of northern lights. That same year the university also established the Meteorological Service of Canada.

- In 1882–83, the first International Polar Year—a scientific fact-gathering organization focused on Canada's Arctic region and later expanded to the Antarctic—was organized.

- The first scientist to record beeps from the *Sputnik 1* satellite was John Chapman and his colleagues at the Defence Research Telecommunications Establishment. Chapman's ongoing efforts in space research earned him a reputation as "the father of the Canadian Space Program."

- Winnipeg's Bristol Aerospace built Black Brant I, the first all-Canadian sounding rocket in 1959. It was launched from Churchill, Manitoba, on September 5, 1959.

- *Alouette I,* launched in 1962, was not only Canada's first satellite into space but it also was only the third in the world to do so. Initially, the satellite was expected to orbit for one year, but it collected data for 10 years before it was retired.

- The first Canadian in space was Marc Garneau. He was a member of the *Challenger* STS-41-G mission, launched on October 5, 1984.

- Canada's first woman in space was Dr. Roberta Bondar. She was part of the team on the space shuttle *Discovery,* mission STS-42, which launched on January 22, 1992.

- In 1972, Telesat Canada established the *ANIK A1* in our country's north. Known as a geostationary communications satellite, used for domestic, non-military purposes, the *ANIK* gave the CBC the power it needed to transmit programming to Canada's northernmost regions. The *ANIK*, named after the Inuit word meaning "little brother," was the "world's first national domestic satellite."

- *ANIK A2* was launched on April 20, 1973, and the third was launched on May 7, 1975. These satellites improved telecommunications throughout the country, and a direct result of these satellites is that "the Stanley Cup and Grey Cup broadcasts could be received in real time in all parts of the country."

- Miller Communications built the first non-Telesat-owned station in 1974 to service the community of Teslin, Yukon.

- The Canadian Space Agency was first formed in 1989. Its mission is to "promote development and advance knowledge of space and to ensure that space science and technology provide social and economic benefits for Canadians."

- Chris Hadfield made his maiden voyage into space in 1995. On April 20, 2001, he completed a second journey and became the first Canadian astronaut to "walk in space."

- Microvariability and Oscillations of Stars (MOST) is Canada's first space telescope. It's about the size of an extra-large suitcase (53 kilograms) and was launched from a Russian nuclear missile in June 2003.

- During the September 2006 *Atlantis* expedition, Steve MacLean became the first Canadian to operate the Canadarm2 in space.

Medicine

The good physician treats the disease; the great physician treats the patient who has the disease.

–William Osler, (1849–1919), Canadian physician

CANADIANS HAVE MADE medical history from the early days of the country's formation, and continue to do so today. Our scientists have made great strides in the field of medical advancements. For example, it was a Canadian who painstakingly developed insulin, thereby giving diabetics a chance at living a normal life, and it was a Canadian who developed the pacemaker.

The medical profession in this country has experienced many growing pains in an effort to define itself. Initially, women with an aptitude for medicine were discouraged, and even criticized, for enrolling in studies and obtaining an education. But that didn't stop those for whom the vocation was of paramount importance, and many travelled to schools in the U.S. to obtain their degrees.

If you think that education made it easier for women to set up a medical practice back on Canadian soil, you're sadly mistaken. It could be said that those in authority persecuted women doctors. Their credentials were repeatedly questioned, not to mention their abilities. And even after the University of Toronto allowed women into lectures, they were treated horribly. Despite it all, brave pioneering women doctors remained steadfast, fought for equality and contributed to the development of the medical practice here and the world over.

Sir William Osler

Ask any medical student to name the father of modern medicine and they're likely to say Sir William Osler. Born in Bond Head, Ontario, on July 12, 1849, Osler's original goal was to follow in his father's footsteps and study to become a member of the Anglican clergy. But after a short time at Toronto's Trinity College, he re-evaluated his goals and transferred into the Toronto School of Medicine. After two years there, he went to Montréal's McGill University, and in 1872 received his medical degree.

While at McGill, Osler recorded the first of his many significant achievements in the world of medicine by creating the first official journal club—a club where members meet regularly to discuss the merits of the latest scientific and medical articles.

Osler's critical mind and focus on giving his best at every moment made him a great doctor. He investigated theories others overlooked; for example, that the health of our psychological state is tied to our physiological well-being, for which he coined the term "psychosomatic." He believed a person's state of mind was critical to a patient's recovery and stressed the importance of bedside practice in the training of medical doctors. This led him to establish the first medical residency system where interns working in real hospital settings could learn by talking directly to their patients and observing their conditions firsthand.

After serving for 10 years as a professor at McGill, Osler moved to the U.S. and took a position as the chair of clinical medicine at Philadelphia's University of Pennsylvania. In 1889 he joined Johns Hopkins University School of Medicine in Baltimore as its first chief of staff.

Osler was also among the first in the field of medicine to fully examine the benefits of laughter in wellness. He even went so far as to cause a lot of levity himself, once writing an article on the "phenomenon of penis captivus" (where the vagina contracts to such an extent during intercourse that the penis cannot be withdrawn, no matter how flaccid it becomes) for the *Philadelphia Medical News* under the pseudonym of Egerton Yorrick Davis. Published in 1884, the article was so convincing that penis captivus catapulted into the realm of urban legend. Strangely enough, one case of the "disease" was reported in 1947 in the *British Medical Journal*. The best part, though, was that the article made people laugh, and in some of his more serious research, he observed how laughter actually helped in a patient's recovery.

Osler was often hailed as the most influential mind in medicine, and though he was made a baronet (a rank of honour below a baron and above a knight) in 1911, he'd likely prefer to be remembered by the readers of his many published works for his quest to live life to the fullest: "Live neither in the past nor in the future, but let each day's work absorb your entire energies, and satisfy your widest ambition."

First Canadian Doctor
to Work in China

Dr. Leonora Howard King was born in Farmersville (now Athens), Ontario, in 1851, and by all accounts was a self-sacrificing young woman from very early on. Although her family was middle class and not wanting for the necessities of life, Leonora was noticeably quiet when it came to asking for anything for herself.

Leonora began her career as a schoolteacher, but the profession didn't satisfy her. Her grandfather and uncle were doctors, and she had a burning desire to study medicine too, but Canadian medical schools wouldn't accept female students then. Of course, anyone with real drive wouldn't let a little thing like that stop them, and Leonora persisted until she was accepted by the Women's Medical College at the University of Michigan in 1872.

She graduated in 1876 and, as with other determined women of her day who travelled to acquire the education they so desperately desired, wasn't allowed to use her newfound knowledge on her return home. It goes without saying that if women in Canada couldn't study medicine back then, they certainly weren't allowed to practice it either.

Thankfully, however, Leonora came to the attention of the Women's Foreign Missionary Society, a branch of the American Methodist Episcopal Missionary Society. Under their umbrella, she became Canada's first female missionary to China, building a medical practice that centred on women and children. Leonora even cared for Lady Li, the wife of a powerful government official of the day, Li Hongzhang, and she lived with the Chinese people from 1877 to the 1920s.

Medical Firsts for Women

Emily Stowe was already an accomplished teacher, and served as Upper Canada's first female principal, when she settled down to have a family in 1856. She and her British immigrant husband John Stowe had three children before John became seriously ill with tuberculosis. Emily's mother was schooled in homeopathic medicine, and with the onset of John's illness, it got Emily pondering the option of studying to become a physician. So in 1865 she applied to the Toronto School of Medicine, only to receive a curt reply saying they didn't admit women and weren't ever likely to do so.

Perturbed but not dissuaded, Emily looked to our neighbours to the south for schooling opportunities and enrolled in the New York Medical College for Women. She graduated two years later with a degree in homeopathic medicine and immediately established a practice on Richmond Street. That action gave her the status of becoming the country's first practicing female physician, but the designation didn't garner her a lot of fanfare. Instead, she was challenged by the Canadian medical establishment of the day. Like any other physician who'd acquired their education outside of Canada, Emily had to take additional courses in this country to qualify as a physician here. Meanwhile, the University of Toronto still wasn't accepting female students.

The battle continued until 1871 when she and Jenny Trout became the "first two women to attend lectures at the Toronto School of Medicine." They still weren't full-fledged medical students, but it was a start.

You would think that the road would be smooth from that moment on, but life at medical school was nothing short of harrowing. The women were taunted and teased until Emily, fed up with it all, returned to her practice. Jenny continued on alone, but eventually transferred to

the Women's Medical College in Pennsylvania. She graduated on March 11, 1875, and became the "first licensed
female physician in Canada."

Emily was by no means beaten, however. She continued to practice medicine, and even faced criminal prose-
cution for performing an alleged abortion—a charge for
which she was acquitted. She also lobbied the College of
Physicians and Surgeons of Ontario until, in 1880, she
was finally granted a medical licence. Emily Stowe was
the second woman in Canada to achieve this milestone.

Frustrated by the male-dominated society that she
perceived was around her, Emily went on to fight for
women's rights and was one of the founding members of
the country's first suffragette group, the Toronto Wom-
en's Literary Guild. She continued to advocate for opportunities for women to study medicine in Canada, and
eventually the University of Toronto reversed its earlier
policies and women were granted the same opportunities
for admission to medical school as their male counterparts.

In 1883, Emily's daughter, Augusta Stowe-Gullen, was
the first woman to graduate with a degree in medicine
from a Canadian medical school.

Inventor of Insulin

More than two million Canadians are thought to have diabetes; a third don't even know they have the disease. Without treatment, high blood sugar levels and malfunctioning metabolism play havoc with a person's health, potentially causing everything from blindness to kidney failure and death. Even today, with the various treatment options available, diabetes is number seven on the causes of death for Canadians, and diabetics still deal with life-altering complications such as lower limb amputations and increased likelihood of heart disease and stroke.

Less than 100 years ago, a person diagnosed with diabetes faced a slow and painful death sentence, but the world of medicine was keeping abreast of the potential causes of the disease. In 1869 a German medical student named Paul Langerhans identified two different systems of cells located in the pancreas. He didn't get much further than that with his research, but his efforts were enough to have these cells named after him, called the Islets of Langerhans. More than 20 years later, in 1893, French researcher Edouard Hedon discovered that the pancreas performed two main functions: it produced digestive juices and regulated carbohydrate metabolism. But it was a research team led by a Canadian that put these and other pieces of information together to understand the pancreas' function in regulating blood sugar.

The quest into the mysteries of diabetes began for Ontario-born Frederick Grant Banting in October 1920, after he read "The Relation of the Islets of Langerhans to Diabetes with Special Reference to Cases of Pancreatic Lithiasis," an article by Moses Barron. It got Banting thinking that if you could extract the internal secretions that the article spoke of, and then inject them into a diabetic patient, it could be a step toward eliminating sugars in the urine.

The revelation was a far cry from anything concrete, but it started what amounted to two years of ongoing research. Banting, however, who was a general practitioner, raised a little ire in the world of medical academe. After all, who was this upstart, and how did he feel qualified to do something so many research specialists before him weren't able to achieve? But he persisted, and sometimes the best way to rid yourself of a pest is to give way.

Banting started his research in a lab at the University of Toronto and was assigned two student researchers. Charles Best stood by his side and, in the end, received credit from Banting himself as the co-discoverer of insulin—the magic formula that changed diabetes from a terminal condition to a chronic one. Dr. John James Rickard Macleod, research supervisor and head of the department where Banting conducted his research, and Dr. James Bertram Collip, an Alberta-based researcher, also lent their expertise to the project. And by the end of 1922, insulin became available to diabetics throughout North America.

Banting and Macleod were awarded the Nobel Prize for Physiology or Medicine in 1923. Banting shared his monetary portion of the prize with Best, and Macleod divided his with Collip.

First Quintuplets

May 28, 1934, should have been a glorious day—a day of prayer for the health and well-being of five identical sisters born two months too early, and celebration for the family who bore them. Worry, of course, was the first response to the birth of the Dionne quintuplets: Annette, Cecile, Emilie, Marie and Yvonne. The sisters were born in Corbeil, Ontario, to Elzire and Olivia Dionne. The chances of birthing identical quintuplets are one in 57 million, and before these babies were born, not a single set of newborn quintuplets survived more than a few days. Therefore, coming into the world with a collective birth weight of 13.6 pounds didn't bode well for the quints' survival.

As each day passed, the quints became stronger, and news of their birth spread. Pretty soon they were known the world over—a distinction that resulted from their mere survival. By default, Dr. Allan Roy Dafoe became the first doctor in the world to successfully deliver quints who had survived.

Because of the babies' frail health, the Ontario government took custody of the girls, raising them in a tourist circus called "Quintland" for the first nine years of their lives. Dr. Dafoe and a staff of nurses cared for the sisters, and according to media reports of the day, they seemed to be well cared for. It didn't occur to the public that it was strange or inhumane that three times each day, the girls were displayed behind a one-way screen, and as many as 6000 people visited Quintland to watch them play. It is reported that the quints brought in as much as a half a billion dollars in the years they lived in Quintland, making them the biggest tourist attraction in the province, surpassing Niagara Falls as a visitor destination.

Sadly, neither the Dionne family nor the quints' trust fund seemed to mirror much of this wealth. If the family was impoverished before, things didn't get any better when the quints returned to the family home, and that poverty followed them into adulthood. In 1965, the sisters wrote their life story in the book *We Were Five*. It afforded them a little financial comfort but substantially less than they needed to survive. In 1995 another book was released, which revealed how the girls were allegedly sexually assaulted by their father and verbally and physically abused by their mother. The seven other Dionne siblings were also called to task for their often-harsh treatment of the quints, an allegation they denied.

Eventually, Annette, Cecile and Yvonne challenged the Ontario government and, after much haggling and severe public backlash, Premier Mike Harris announced the three remaining sisters would be granted $4 million in compensation payments. The women agreed to the settlement.

Of the five, Emilie was the first to die. She passed away in 1954 at the age of 20 after suffering a seizure. Marie died at age 35 in 1970 of a blood clot, and Yvonne passed away in 2001 from cancer; she was 67. Annette and Cecile presently live in Montréal.

Other Famous Births

- On January 6 and 7, 2007, sextuplets were born at the BC Women's Hospital and Health Centre. The four boys and two girls were at just 25 weeks gestation when they came into the world, each weighing between one pound, six ounces and one pound, twelve ounces. The parents, well aware of the need to protect their children from the same media fiasco the Dionne quintuplets faced, refused to reveal their names to the public. The chances of giving birth to sextuplets are one in 4.7 billion, and chances of survival even slimmer. By January 23, 2007, two of the six Vancouver-born babies had passed away.

- On October 25, 2007, Krista and Tatiana Hogan were born in Vancouver, making history as being Canada's only set of craniopagus twins (conjoined twins with fused skulls). At birth they were a combined weight of 12 pounds, 11 ounces, and it was clear early on that they seemed to experience each other's pain and pleasure—if you tickled one of the little girl's feet, both girls would laugh. Because the girls share parts of their brains, separation is not medically possible at this time.

- In November 1999, Western Canada witnessed the birth of its first set of quintuplets when Yvonne and Rob Gilmour delivered their babies in a Saskatoon hospital. Madisson, Alexandra, Sarah, Simon and Ryan were 11 weeks early when they made their grand entry.

- On December 17, 1982, Carrie Dawn, Jennie Lee, Mary Beth and Patty Ann were born to Pat and Martin Steeves of Calgary. Although other quadruplets had been born in Canada, the Steeves babies were the first identical quads born in the country. Instances of such a birth occur statistically only one in 13 million.

The girls, now adults, never thought they'd live to see another set of siblings that fit into their category, but on August 12, 2007, Karen and J.P. Jepp welcomed their identical quadruplets into the world. Autumn, Brooke, Calissa and Dahlia are all doing well as of this writing. And though this kind of birth is extremely rare, keep in mind that the Jepps also reside in Calgary—you figure out those odds.

- On May 29, 1902, in what is now Wolseley, Saskatchewan (Saskatchewan was not a province until 1905), Walter and Jane Hall welcomed their twin girls, Sarah and Ellen, into the world. While that in itself may not seem out of the ordinary, what is extraordinary is that, as of this writing, they are still alive. Family and friends in Winnipeg, the city where they spent their formative years, hosted a 105th birthday celebration for the sisters in 2007 (though Ellen wasn't able to attend because of illness). The milestone made them the longest living twins in Canada, according to the *Guinness Book of World Records*, and currently the longest living twins in the world. They credit their longevity to "clean living."

First Use of Cobalt-60 in Canada

"Great minds think alike." As sometimes happens, two or three individuals simultaneously work toward the same end, completely oblivious to one another. Sometimes they even come up with the same results at almost the same time. In this story, such a coincidence resulted in the development of Cobalt-60, a "radioactive form of the metal cobalt" used in a revolutionary new cancer treatment.

As early as 1945, British researchers were discussing the need for a radiation source stronger than what was being used in x-ray treatments for cancer patients. Around the same time, University of Saskatchewan's physics department was being hailed as a Canadian leader in the field of nuclear physics, leading the way for our country's first betatron—a machine used in x-ray treatment—to be installed in its associate hospital. But it was expensive and ineffectual, and Saskatchewan researchers knew they had to push for the development of Cobalt-60, which occurs when Cobalt-59 is secured in a neutron field, destabilizing it and producing gamma radiation. While Cobalt-59 was going through the transition process, engineers were busy developing the "world's first non-commercial Cobalt-60 machine." R.F. Errington and D.I. Green from Eldorado Mining and Refining Limited designed the Ontario unit, and Dr. Harold Johns designed the Saskatchewan unit, focusing on protecting healthcare providers from unnecessary exposure to the rays and regulating the amount of radiation delivered at any given time.

By then, three batches of Cobalt-60 were produced at Canada's nuclear reactor in Chalk River, Ontario. One batch went to the Victoria Hospital in London, a second to University of Saskatchewan researchers and the third, originally destined for the U.S., wasn't sent out until a year later.

With both Canadian teams possessing this exciting new medical marvel, each was eager to test their theory on patients with malignant tumours. According to Dr. Johns' colleague, Dr. Sylvia Fedoruk: "The machine was actually quite easy to operate...because of the intense radiation generated from the Cobalt-60, the machine was very good for treating deep-seated tumours in the bladder, cervix and lungs."

Two brave cancer patients agreed to undergo the first Cobalt treatments. In August 1951, Victoria Hospital in London was the first to use the treatment on a patient. Two months later, in October 1951, Saskatchewan's machine was ready to go, and a 43-year-old mother of four, Molly Birtsch, was the first to receive the therapy. Sadly, the London patient died shortly after treatment, but Molly Birtsch beat the odds and lived. Despite the loss of one of the two first patients, the use of Cobalt-60 in the treatment of tumours was considered successful, and the technology began to be used the world over.

The unit installed in Saskatchewan was used for 21 years before it was finally replaced by another machine, this one designed by Atomic Energy of Canada Ltd. During its years of service it was used in the treatment of 6728 patients.

More than 50 years after its inception, the National Research Universal Reactor (NRU) at Chalk River is still in operation, though not without its controversy. In August 2006, the Canadian Nuclear Safety Commission required upgrades to several parts of the plant in order to meet safety standards. Most of these proposed upgrades focused on the facility's ability to better withstand earthquakes, which have historically occurred in the area. Without these upgrades an earthquake could result in

a "loss of coolant," causing a disaster similar to the Three
Mile Island incident in 1979. The proposed upgrades were
expected to take about five days to complete, and on
November 18, 2007, the plant was shut down for the purpose. However, during the process it was noticed that
other safety modifications hadn't been made, and the
five-day shutdown continued with no end in sight. Since
NRU produces most of the world's supply of radioisotopes
and the nuclear isomer technetium-99, both necessary in
the medical treatment of cancer, as well as in the treatment and diagnosis of other conditions such as heart disease, the move immediately caused an international
shortage. Canada's Conservative government, led by
Prime Minister Stephen Harper, made the controversial
and, as his government called it, "emergency" decision to
reopen the plant for 120 days in December 2007, even
though the upgrades weren't complete. While the production of molybdenum-99 and technetium-99m are
once again underway, Atomic Energy of Canada, which
owns and operates the plant, is continuing on with the
planned upgrades.

First Birth from Frozen Eggs

Although it's not uncommon for individuals these days to forego having children, most young couples still want to have at least one child, according to Census Canada's 2007 estimates, and about 10.75 births per 1000 people are recorded every year.

For couples struggling with fertility issues, living in Canada is a good thing. Our country leads the way in a number of areas in fertility research, and in 2005, Canada recorded a world first with the birth on April 29 of a baby boy who had been conceived from a frozen egg.

The eight-pound infant (names were withheld from the media at the family's request), born to a 26-year-old mother at the McGill Reproductive Centre at the McGill University Health Centre in Montréal, was the "first successful birth in Canada resulting from frozen eggs."

Eggs are frozen for a number of reasons: the mother is undergoing medical treatment that could affect her fertility, or the mother wants to wait to have children, which, statistics show, also reduces fertility. But freezing eggs is difficult to do without causing irreparable damage. Eggs have high water content and must go through a rapid-freezing process called "vitrification," a procedure developed by Dr. Seang Lin Tan, chair of the Department of Obstetrics and Gynecology, and Dr. Ri-Cheng Chian, the scientific director of the McGill Reproductive Centre. This super-cooling method reduces the likelihood that ice crystals will form inside the egg and increases the survival rate for the eggs to 90 percent—an amazing feat since as many as 85 percent of eggs frozen for future use do not survive the freezing. At the time of the first miraculous birth in 2005, 15 patients had undergone embryo transfer, resulting in seven pregnancies.

~oOo~

First Mother to Daughter Egg Harvest

In April 2007, the McGill Reproductive Centre made medical news again in a controversial first that had a mother freezing her eggs for her daughter's potential, future use. Montréal lawyer Melanie Boivin approached Dr. Seang Lin Tan, the centre's director, with the proposal in 2005, hoping that if he took on the case, her frozen eggs could give her seven-year-old daughter the chance to someday have a family. It was something that wouldn't otherwise be possible for Boivin's daughter, who was diagnosed with Turner's Syndrome, and infertility is common in women with the condition.

McGill and Boivin faced some criticism from ethicists who questioned the procedure from the child's point of view, suggesting the "scrambling of the generations" could cause the baby—who'd be both sister and daughter to her birth mother—psychological confusion. Dr. Tan took the concerns to the McGill ethics committee who, after thoughtful consideration, approved the procedure. Boivin told reporters that she and her husband thought long and hard about their decision, but decided the procedure was no different than giving their daughter a kidney should she have required one. And when reporters asked Boivin who the baby's "real mother" would be should their daughter decide to use one of the frozen eggs, Boivin's answer was simple—the woman raising a child is that child's "real mother."

Other Birthing Firsts

- Contraceptives have been around for a long time, but in 1882 the Canadian government criminalized the advertisement or sale of contraceptives.

- Dr. Elizabeth Bagshaw set up the country's first, and illegal, birth control clinic in Hamilton, Ontario. From 1932 to 1966 she met with patients every Friday afternoon and provided them with information and contraceptives, such as condoms, despite opposition from other medical personnel and church officials. When she retired in 1976 at the age of 95, she still had a practice of 50 patients and was considered the oldest practicing physician in the country.

- It wasn't until 1961 that Canadian doctors were first allowed to prescribe the birth control pill. A smart shopper back then might have been able to find condoms and other contraceptives discretely hidden away on drug store shelves, but selling them was still technically illegal.

- Canada legalized birth control in 1969. Abortions were also legalized, but were only approved if the mother's health was in jeopardy.

- The country's first test-tube baby, Robby Reid, was born on Christmas Day 1983 in a Vancouver hospital.

Random Medical Firsts

- Canada's first weekly medical journal, the short-lived *Canadian Medical Times: A Weekly Journal of Medical Science, News, and Politics,* was published from July 5 to December 27, 1873.

- The Canadian Medical Hall of Fame welcomed the induction of its first saint in 2003. Saint Marguerite d'Youville was honoured for her work as the founder of the Sisters of Charity of the Hôpital General de Montréal, but her influence was widespread. The Sisters of Charity of Montréal (also known as "Grey Nuns") established other sister communities, including those in St. Hyacinthe, Ottawa, Québec, Pembroke, Winnipeg and Edmonton. Marguerite d'Youville was also the first native Canadian to be declared a saint.

- Dr. John Callaghan of the University of Alberta Hospital performed Canada's first open heart surgery in September 1956. He was just 32 years old at the time.

- Canada's first heart transplant recipient was Albert Murphy of Chomedy, Québec. The 59-year-old retired butcher received his gift of life on May 31, 1968, making him the 18th person in the world to undergo the procedure. He'd received the heart of a 38-year-old mother who'd died of a brain hemorrhage. But when Murphy died, 41 hours after the operation, it was thought the heart was too small to maintain the man's blood pressure.

- In 2005, Laurentian University opened its doors to a new program that was a first for the country—Canada's first rural medical school. The idea for the program stemmed from rural doctors, especially ones with unique populations, who needed a broader education than the typical medical program usually offers. The Northern Ontario School of Medicine offers teaching and research opportunities at Thunder Bay and Sudbury. The focus of study includes an emphasis on First Nations and francophone cultures, the needs of small and northern villages and the challenges of practicing medicine in remote locations.

- Dr. Frederick Montizambert became Canada's first federal Director General of Public Health in 1899.

- Dr. John G. FitzGerald, in conjunction with the University of Toronto, founded Connaught Laboratories in 1914. That's where Canada's "first safe, effective, Canadian-made rabies vaccine and diphtheria anti-toxin" were developed.

- Québec City's Dr. Jean Dussault (1941–2003) saved hundreds of thousands of children around the world from the stigma of mental retardation through his development of a "neonatal diagnostic test for congenital hypothyroidism." The condition affects one in 4000 births. With a simple pinprick to the heel, an infant's blood is tested for the condition, which when treated early, is reversible.

- Dr. Hans Selye (1907–82) of McGill University developed the theory "General Adaptation Syndrome" (GAS) in 1936. GAS basically outlines how stress, the result of mental, physiological, anatomical or physical stimuli on our bodies, is a major factor in disease. Selye was the first physician to recognize stress in a "medical context," and he received worldwide recognition for his lifetime of research on the topic.

- Dr. Maude Elizabeth Seymour Abbott (1869–1940) was the country's first "honorary" female doctor who, despite entering the world of medicine at a time when women weren't accepted into the field, earned a worldwide reputation as the "inventor of the first international classification system for congenital heart disease."

- Dr. Charlotte Whitehead Ross made her way to the windy city of Winnipeg in 1881 with a medical degree from the Women's Medical College of Pennsylvania to her credit and a husband and family to care for. But Winnipeg was just a pit stop. The family settled in the small community of Whitemouth, Manitoba, and in doing so Dr. Ross became the first white woman to live in the region. She was also the first doctor (and only one for many years) in the area, and although she worked without a licence for her entire 27-year practice in Manitoba, she was granted one posthumously in 1993 and officially recognized as the province's first woman doctor.

- Dr. Maud Menten received almost immediate, though begrudging, recognition as the country's first official woman doctor. She graduated from the University of Toronto in 1913, a full 38 years after Dr. Ross graduated, but Dr. Menten's qualifications were recognized because they were achieved in Canada. The same year that Dr. Menten graduated, she and Dr. Leonor Michaelis developed the "Michaelis-Menten equation"—a mathematical formula to help doctors "analyze their observations and descriptions of biological reactions."

- In 1992, Dr. Roberta Bondar became Canada's first woman in space. Her main objective in the mission was to study the effect of weightlessness on the human body and the "growth of plants without gravity."

- BLISSYMBOLICS, a graphic communications system to help physically challenged persons communicate, was invented by Canadian Charles Bliss in 1949 and was first used with children suffering from cerebral palsy in 1971.

- In the mid-1980s, 12-year-old Rachel Zimmerman of Ontario took Charles Bliss' invention a step further with the development of the BLISSYMBOL Printer—a software program that translates the symbols being pointed to on the BLISSYMBOLICS unit into written words. This helps the user journal their thoughts or write emails. The project, which began as a school science fair entry, earned Rachel a silver medal at the nationwide World Exhibition of Achievement of Young Inventors, and a YTV Television Youth Achievement Award.

- In 1913, Dr. Wilfred Bigelow Sr. established the first private health clinic in Canada.

- The first time heart valves were transplanted in patients in Canada, or anywhere in the world, was at Toronto General Hospital in 1956.

- Dr. Wilfred Bigelow Jr. was a man of firsts when it came to the world of cardiac medicine. He was the first to introduce a technique using hypothermia in open heart surgery. In 1950, he and colleague Dr. John Callaghan (who went on to accumulate more medical milestones when he performed the first open heart surgery in 1956), along with John Hopps, an electrical engineer, helped develop the first electronic pacemaker. That first, 1950-style prototype was too large to implant into a human chest, but another version was made in 1958 and successfully implanted.

- The first kidney transplant performed between identical twins took place at Montréal's Royal Victoria Hospital. The year was 1958.

- St. Paul's Hospital in Saskatoon was the site of the country's first hemodialysis treatment (a procedure that removes waste and toxins from the blood, often necessary in patients with kidney failure) in 1963.

- The world's first successful lung transplant took place at the Toronto General Hospital in 1983.

- In 1986, Toronto General Hospital was also the site of the world's first-ever and successful double-lung transplant. The recipient was Ann Harrison.

- The country's first heart-lung transplant took place in 1983 at the University Hospital in London, Ontario.

- The University Hospital in London was in the spotlight again in 1990, this time garnering international attention as the first hospital in the world to perform a "combined liver and bowel transplant." Two years later, in 1992, the hospital was the first in Canada to complete a multi-organ transplant. The patient received a new liver, small bowel, stomach and pancreas. The first "adult-to-adult living liver transplant" in the country was completed in 2000, also at the University Hospital.

- Toronto resident Wendy Murphy was propelled into action after viewing footage of Mexico's disastrous earthquake of 1985. While she watched rescue workers passing newborns barely alive through the rubble of a demolished hospital, she came up with an idea for a unique, six-baby stretcher. She named her invention the WEEVAC 6.

- Insulin-dependent patients with hard-to-control type 1 diabetes were offered a new way of managing their disease after researchers at the University of Alberta, located in Edmonton, Alberta, reported their experimentation with islet transplantation in the June 2000 *New England Journal of Medicine*. The procedure they developed, called the Edmonton Protocol, built on the idea of transplanting healthy pancreatic islets into type 1 diabetics, thereby restricting or even eliminating the need for insulin injections. Sixty-five patients were chosen for the first procedure of its kind, and five years later, 10 percent of those patients still did not require insulin injections. In some of the remaining cases the pancreatic islets became sterile, and patients returned to their pre-transplant management schedule. But in many of these transplant cases, though patients were still dealing with the disease, they were better able to manage it, reducing their dependence on insulin.

- The MP3 player we all know as a device for recording and listening to music might have a few other uses in the near future. In 2007, University of Alberta researchers respirologist Dr. Neil Skjodt and audiologist Bill Hodgetts claim the "quality, clarity and purity of the loud sounds" produced by an MP3 player are superior to those produced by a stethoscope. To test their theory, they provided respirologists in training with MP3 breathing recordings from patients experiencing different symptoms to see if they could differentiate between them all. Skjodt reported, "they were better at recognizing common combinations of breath sounds and wheezing using the device, though more subtle sounds were still a problem." The device is being considered for listening to "heart and bowel sounds as well."

- Dr. Lap-Chee Tsui, a molecular biologist with Toronto's Hospital for Sick Children, made medical history when on May 9, 1989, he first discovered the gene for cystic fibrosis—a disease that kills one in 2000 Canadians.

Military

*Very little is known about the War of 1812 because the
Americans lost it.*

–Eric Nicol (1919–), humorist and writer

THE QUESTION OF how to go about protecting our country's
interests has been of paramount concern from the time
explorers first began settling in Canada. French and British occupation in various corners of the country initially
provided protection for their interests. But when the British gained control of the country, they took over military
responsibility.

With Confederation, the military became the responsibility of the Canadian government. And like anything
else, the citizens of this country have had to grow into
that new obligation.

Canada is disproportionately larger, geographically
speaking, than its population. And that fact directly
affects the size and power of our military presence in the
world. However, this doesn't mean Canada hasn't made a
significant impact both within the country and worldwide. Canadian women made international military history when Major Deanna Brasseur became the world's
first female fighter pilot. Canada could have ruled the
skies with the Avro Arrow too, but the promising project
died, shrouded in mystery.

What follows are a few highlights about how our military has formed and a brief collection of our accomplishments. It is by no means a definitive accounting of all our
military high points.

First Jetliner

Sometimes greatness isn't enough to secure a person's future, and if you ever need proof of this, just take a look at the Avro Arrow. At its unveiling, it was considered by many as "the greatest moment in the history of Canadian aviation technology," and yet it disappeared from the radar as if it had never existed.

It all began after World War II. Avro Canada Ltd. (then A.V. Roe Aircraft company) wanted to build a jetliner, thinking that it would make air travel faster. Previously planes were propeller driven. In April 1950, the company proved it could accomplish this when its CF-100 made its record-breaking one-hour flight between Toronto and New York City—that was less than half the time a typical flight of the day took. The event marked the first time in North American history that a passenger jet flew over the continent. And the three crewmembers and three passengers on board also delivered the world's first airmail that day.

The federal government was looking to expand its jet-fighter capabilities and contacted the company responsible for manufacturing the Arrow. The end result was the CF-102. It was unveiled on October 4, 1957, boasting a speed of MACH 2+ and capable of shooting down any Russian planes threatening Canadian airspace during the Cold War, which was raging loud and long at the time. CBC Radio broadcasted this news report during the Arrow's first flight:

> At 9:52 AM on March 25, 1958, Arrow RL-201 roars into the skies above Malton for the Avro Arrow's first test flight. Three kilometres below, all nonessential Avro staff pour out of the plant to watch their plane circle overhead. Some 35 minutes later, the Arrow touches

down and comes to a halt, braking parachutes trailing
behind. Test pilot Janusz Zurakowski, who is given a
hero's welcome, complains only that the cockpit has no
clock.

Yet despite the flight being a success, and another five planes being built, newly elected Prime Minister John Diefenbaker scrapped the project on February 20, 1959. The decision put thousands of people out of work, and a further instruction to destroy all the planes in all stages of production, blueprints and all, cost the federal government an astonishing $400 million.

Why the Canadian government called a halt to what could have been our country's most crowning achievement in aviation technology remains a mystery.

World's First Female Fighter Pilot

Sometimes you just know what you were born to do for the rest of your life, and you work hard to attain it. For Major Deanna Brasseur, her dream of becoming a fighter pilot with the Canadian military wasn't simply a tough challenge—it seemed an unreachable goal.

Born in 1953, Deanna had always been fascinated by planes and flying. Some might suggest it was a natural inclination because her father, Lieutenant Colonel Lyn Brasseur, was in the Royal Canadian Air Force. The young Deanna was no doubt exposed to the awe-inspiring power of military fighter jets at a young age.

Still, she never thought anything would come of it. In June 1989 she told the *Ottawa Citizen*, "When I was going through high school, women were supposed to be nurses or teachers, and you only did that until you got married. Then you were supposed to stay home." But early on Brasseur knew she couldn't follow those arbitrary expectations.

In 1972 she dropped out of university and joined the Canadian military, sticking to the kinds of jobs typically delegated to women. But she wasn't happy doing that either. After just a year working as a typist in a dental office at CFB Winnipeg, she enrolled in the officers' training program, completed her requirements and took a job as a weapons controller. It still wasn't where Brasseur wanted to be, but it was certainly a step in the right direction.

In 1979 she took another step when she was one of four women accepted into a basic pilot training program. Two years later she was one of three women who completed the program and got their "wings." This, in itself, made Canadian military history, but Brasseur didn't stop there. A year later she became the first female flight instructor, taking her post at the 2 Canadian Forces Flying Training School in Moose Jaw, Saskatchewan. She continued to chalk up the firsts by being named the first female flight commander at Base Flight Cold Lake, Alberta, in 1986.

The list of accomplishments during Brasseur's 21-year career is long and impressive, but her crowning achievement came in 1989 when she became one of two women to qualify on the CF-18 Hornet. Only 10 percent of pilots ever qualify to fly a CF-18 fighter jet, which can reach speeds of MACH 1.8, or almost twice the speed of sound. This was a first for Canada and a first for women across the world.

Brasseur had racked up 2500 flying hours by the time she retired in 1994. In 1998 she was inducted into the International Organization of Women Pilots Forest of Friendship in Atchison, Kansas. That same year she was named to *Maclean's* Annual Honour Roll, for "speaking out about the topic of rape and sexual abuse in the military"—her rise to the top didn't come without personal hardships, as she herself had experienced similar abuse. In 1999 she was made a Member of the Order of Canada.

Other Military Firsts

- The first major war involving British and French colonies in North America was the War of the Spanish Succession, which raged on in Europe from 1702 to 1713 and inadvertently affected colonies in the New World.

- The Seven Years' War took place between 1754 and 1761. It was the first, large-scale conflict involving British and French colonies on Canadian soil.

- *Hosti Acie Nominati*, Latin for "named by the enemy in battle," is the regimental motto of the Royal Winnipeg Rifles. The infantry regiment of the Canadian Forces was established in Winnipeg in 1883. Its first commander was Lieutenant Colonel William Nassau Kennedy.

- Following Confederation, a Canadian military began to take shape, but because Canada was still a British colony, our forces joined theirs whenever the need arose, such as during the Second Boer War, World War I and World War II.

- Canada's military was called in to help Britain for the first time in 1884. Its mission was to rescue Major-General Charles Gordon from the Mahdi uprising.

- Discussions about the establishment of a Royal Canadian Navy began in 1909, but nothing concrete came of it until May 4, 1910, with the passing of the Naval Service Act. The official name was the Naval Service of Canada (also known as the Canadian Naval Forces). Rear-Admiral Charles Kingsmill was its first director. The name was changed again on January 30, 1911, when it became the Royal Canadian Navy—King George V conferred the "royal" title on August 29 of that year. The navy continued on in its own identity until 1968, when the navy, air force and army ground services united to form the Canadian Forces (CF).

- The first two ships commissioned to Canada's new navy were the *Rainbow*, which came on board on August 4, 1910, and the HMS *Niobe*, commissioned on September 6, 1910.

- The first two submarines added to the fleet were commissioned on August 7, 1914.

- The Royal Canadian Air Force was formed in 1924. The first Canadian air squadron in action took flight on August 15, 1940.

- The Snowbirds, the flight demonstration team of the CF, was formed on November 11, 1942. The air component of the CF was originally called the 431 Bomber Squadron, and its mission was to fly bombing operations from England. The squadron disbanded in 1945, but reconvened for a time on January 18, 1954, when pilots took to the skies, demonstrating how the new F-86 jet performed. That group disbanded on October 1, 1954, but were recalled to duty from time to time for further demonstrations, until on April 1, 1978, a permanent but independent 431 Air Demonstration Squadron was formed.

- The demonstration arm of the CF first adopted the name "Snowbirds" during an air show at CFB Moose Jaw on July 11, 1971.

- Since World War I, Canada had adopted a policy of multilateralism, which means, as a country, we only go to war "within large multinational coalitions." Examples include the Korean War, the Gulf War and Afghanistan.

- In 1990, Canada was one of the first countries to condemn the invasion of Kuwait, and the CF put some muscle behind that stand by sending the first warship to Kuwait Harbor at the close of the war in 1992. The HMCS *Huron* was responsible for enforcing sanctions.

- During World War I, the remains of an unidentified Canadian soldier were discovered and buried in France and labelled the "Tomb of the Unknown Soldier." In May 2000, the soldier's body was exhumed and moved to a tomb near the National War Memorial in Ottawa, making it Canada's official "Tomb of the Unknown Soldier."

- Canada's first female soldier to die in combat was Captain Nichola Goddard. She was serving in the First Regiment Royal Canadian Horse Artillery in Afghanistan when she was killed on May 17, 2006.

Food and Drink

Much as I enjoy writing and teaching, they box me in.
In the kitchen I take wings.

–Madame Jehane Benoit (1904–87), chef and writer

WITH THE VAST amount of ethnic diversity Canada prides itself in, it's little wonder we've done amazingly well when it comes to making our mark on the food industry. Poutine, and the cocktail favourite, the Bloody Caesar, are only two examples among our long list of originals. Canadians score top marks for some of the best products—just sink your teeth into Ganong chocolates or one of Laura Secord's tasty treats. We've also added to the variety of apples available with the development of the McIntosh and Spartan apples. And who hasn't heard of the name Kraft—he was originally Canadian, by the way.

But creative cuisine isn't our only claim to fame; food, after all, is above all else sustenance—the means to survival. Our wheat crops have been attacked by natural conditions such as rust and fungus, and Canadian agroscientists came to the rescue by developing disease-resistant wheat varieties. Canadians figured out how to freeze fish and create dried potato flakes, offering consumers products with a longer shelf life. And our scientists also invented Pablum, which provided nutrition to infants and toddlers who, in the early part of the 20th century, were dying from malnutrition. For busy Canadians looking for healthier fast-food options, Yves Veggie Cuisine came up with burgers and hot dogs with a difference.

First "Chocolate Family"

We all look forward to the sweet treats that come along with any festive season—chocolate-filled cinnamon sticks (better known as "Chicken Bones") at Christmas, hollow (and solid) chocolate bunnies at Easter or the cream-filled chocolates lining the heart-shaped boxes on Valentine's Day. Sweets have been around for more than 4000 years, but these treats are among a long list of candies and chocolates developed in the maritime community of St. Stephen, New Brunswick.

On May 8, 1873, brothers James and Gilbert Ganong opened G.W. (for Gilbert White) Ganong, Commission Merchant, Etc., a general store with a twist. Previously, however, both brothers had been doing other things with their lives. James, the older of the two, travelled the New England countryside selling biscuits and crackers while Gilbert taught at Carleton with the hope of returning to school someday to study medicine. Yet after some discussion, the two decided to go into business together. Gilbert would run the store while James continued in his travelling sales job. When the store turned enough profit to provide for both families, James would quit travelling and work alongside Gilbert.

Although they didn't initially plan on starting a candy-making business, the idea took form fairly early on in the brothers' enterprise. Wanting to make their store stand out from the rest, the pair brought in a number of specialty items, like candy. But Gilbert didn't like the poor quality of the Canadian candy he received, and the tariffs attached to the import of American candy made it too expensive to stock. By 1874 they approached Charles M. Holt, a local confectioner, to join forces with them, and that's how Canada's oldest and only large-scale, family-owned confectionary began.

Part of the company's success was their ability to attract experts to their business. Frank Sparhawk, a hard-candy specialist from the States, joined the Ganongs and was the mastermind behind the company's first original product developed sometime in the 1890s—the chocolate-filled, satiny-pink cinnamon candy called Chicken Bones. Folks out east still say, "It wouldn't be Christmas without Chicken Bones." A few years later, in 1895, the company followed up that success by placing a ball of hard candy at the end of a wooden skewer and calling it the All-Day Sucker.

A stubborn Jersey cow was the impetus behind the Ganongs' creation of the Jersey milk chocolate bar. The children of the family, thrilled with the cow's antics, thought it a great idea to make some chocolate from the Jersey's milk. In 1910, using a blend of milk, chocolate and assorted nuts, the "world's first five-cent chocolate bar" was born. This first bar remained on the market for 31 years before it was replaced by Pal-o-Mine—Ganong candy-maker Ed Boseina developed the bar when he was asked to "make a bar that felt like a piece of cheese when you bit into it, not too soft, not too firm."

The Ganongs were also leaders when it came to inventive packaging. Theirs was the first Canadian company to wrap their product in cellophane. And in 1906, the company invited a young Harry MacPhail to start the Home Paper Box Company within the Ganong chocolate factory. It was MacPhail who designed the first, cardboard, heart-shaped Valentine box in 1932.

While in today's market the company is a relatively small competitor against the multinationals of Rowntree and Hershey, Ganong continues to grow and invent new taste-tempting treats and remains one of our nation's sweet success stories.

First in Apples

Humankind has enjoyed the sweet, juicy crunch of apples for thousands of years. The Greeks were growing apple varieties as far back as the 300s, and by the 1600s, orchards were found throughout Europe.

French settlers introduced apples to Canada as a crop back in the early 1600s when they planted the first apple trees in Nova Scotia. As settlers moved west, the planted apple trees in other provinces, but they were still European varieties. It wasn't until 1811 that John McIntosh bought a farm in Dundas County, near Ottawa, and discovered a small orchard of 20 apple trees in the nearby woods. All but one died when he tried to move them closer to his home, and that one tree not only survived, but it thrived. In 1870, John's son Allan used the seedlings from that tree to plant the first red apple nursery. He transported grafts of the original tree to other farmers' trees in nearby areas and essentially founded the McIntosh apple industry. Every McIntosh apple tree in the world is directly descended from that one, surviving tree.

Apples in general are considered the world's most popular fruit; a fact certainly supported by the economic impact the apple industry has in this country. Today, Canada's apple crops draw in more than $175 million a year, making it the most important fruit crop in the nation.

First Inventor of Pablum

Working with sick children is a difficult profession. It's hard watching youngsters struggle with illness. But watching babies die of something preventable is especially agonizing. In the early part of the 20th century, the nutritional value in grain cereals wasn't adequate to feed growing babies, many of whom died from malnutrition. A lack of refrigeration was another problem. Mothers often cooked large portions of hot cereals, and because the leftovers were often left out, the resulting bacteria caused youngsters to become ill. So in 1929, Drs. Theodore Drake, Frederick Tisdall and Alan Brown, all of the Hospital for Sick Children in Toronto, joined forces to try to come up with a solution. They needed a product that could be quickly and easily made up in small batches and required no refrigeration. By 1931 they'd come up with two options: the Sunwheat biscuit loaded with nutrients from wheat meal, oatmeal and other grains; and a dry, flaky cereal that mothers could simply mix with warm water and serve. In addition, these products were free of eggs and dairy and other foods thought to cause allergies. The biscuit was perfect for toddlers, especially those who were teething, while the cereal, which they named Pablum, was ideal for infants.

Pablum, so named after the Latin word *pabulum* (pab-you-lum), meaning "foodstuff," was initially marketed by the company Mead Johnson, and royalties for the formula was donated back to the Hospital for Sick Children Pediatric Research Foundation.

Frozen Vittles

Freezing fresh food for use later on was nothing new to the Native people of the North. After a successful seal hunt or fishing expedition, they often packed away parcels of food for another day—it lasted longer when it was frozen and could be thawed before eating.

The Biological Board of Canada (a precursor to the Fisheries Research Board), which was established in 1912 and located in Halifax, decided to do a little research into the idea of freezing food and its possibilities in the marketplace. It took two years of research and experimentation, but in 1929 a marine scientist named Archibald Huntsman came up with a way to artificially replicate what Canada's northernmost residents accomplished naturally. For the first time ever, a frozen fish product called "Ice Fillets" was packaged and sold to eager Canadian consumers.

Sadly, the fishing industry and producers of the day weren't as quick to catch on to the benefits of this modern marvel, and they soon lost interest in backing Huntsman's invention. Two years later, however, U.S. Colonel Clarence Birdseye started marketing his own fast-freeze methods and claimed the invention for the Americans. (To be fair, Birdseye had been researching the issue as far back as 1917 but did not market his product until almost a year after Huntsman's Ice Fillets first hit store shelves.)

Other Firsts for Food and Drink

- Let's face it. We all live busy lives, and in the midst of rushing children home from school and off again to hockey or figure skating, supper is at times a necessary fast fix. But before you pop that frozen pizza into the microwave or oven, why not try a healthier, all-vegetable option. Québec chef Yves Potvin took on the challenge of freshening up fast food with meat-free options, and in 1985 he introduced the world to Yves Veggie Cuisine—vegetable and soy-based wieners, burgers, bacon and pepperoni.

- No one knows the name of the man who first sprinkled cheese curds over French fries and smothered the lot with gravy, but it is known he was from Québec and that in the 1950s he invented the popular fast food called poutine.

- And speaking of cheese, what aficionado of the product hasn't heard of J.L. Kraft? Born in Stevensville, Ontario, and raised on the family's dairy farm, the youngster grew into a culinary maverick. His early work experience as a grocery clerk gave him an understanding of the shelf life of cheese and a desire to offer consumers cheese that was always fresh and flavourful. With that in mind, a young J.L. moved to Chicago in 1903, invested $65 and started peddling cheese from a rented wagon. By 1909 four of his brothers joined him and together they purchased a factory in Stockton, Illinois, and the family legacy was born. Within six years they'd started making the world's first processed cheese and selling the product in small tins. J.L. patented his new product in 1916.

- Ginger beer has been around as an alcoholic drink since the 1700s, but the champagne of ginger ales—non-alcoholic all the way—is another Canadian accomplishment. Canada Dry ginger ale was patented in 1904 after years of research conducted by a chemist and pharmacist named John J. McLaughlin. He'd played with the recipe from 1890, after he opened a soda water manufacturing plant in Toronto. The Canadian soda king first produced ginger ale at that plant on Sherbourne Street. The soda made its debut in the U.S. in 1919, when it was first shipped to New York. In 1921 a second subsidiary plant was opened in Manhattan.

- The McIntosh isn't the only uniquely Canadian apple variety. The Spartan apple is another Canadian invention. Dr. R.C. Palmer developed the apple cultivar in 1926 at what was then known as "the Canadian Apple Research Station in Summerland, British Columbia."

- Folks who like a little spicy kick to their cocktails might be interested to know that the fiery Caesar was a Canadian invention. Similar to a Bloody Mary, a Caesar is made up of tomato juice, vodka and Worcestershire sauce, but an Alberta-born bartender named Walter Chell decided to spice it up a little. In the 1960s he added crushed clams, a dash of something spicy, garnished it with a celery stick and created the Bloody Caesar so many love to indulge in to this day.

- Thomas Ahearn wasn't just the founder of the Ottawa Electric Railway Company and a diehard businessman, he also was an inventor whose creation touches absolutely everyone who has a home with a fully equipped kitchen. In 1882 he invented the electric cooking range and 10 years later reputedly became the first person to prepare a meal on an electric stove which he built in the Windsor Hotel in Montréal.

- In 1913, another chocolatier, Frank P. O'Connor, shared his unique talent at creating sweet treats. Most of us know of his enterprise as Laura Secord Chocolates. Legend has it he named his enterprise after the heroine of the War of 1812, because her name represented "courage, loyalty and devotion to Canadians." Today there are almost 200 Laura Secord shops in Canada, and the company is now headquartered in the U.S.

- In 1916, a rust-type of fungus invaded and destroyed Canadian wheat crops. The devastation led Manitoba's Margaret Newton to develop a rust-resistant strain of wheat in 1917. Five years later she also became the first woman in the country "to earn a PhD in agriculture science."

- Halloween enthusiasts might be interested to know that Howard Dill of Windsor, Nova Scotia, invented the mother of all pumpkins, Dill's Atlantic Giant. The giant jack-o-lantern canvas made its debut sometime in the 1950s.

- Edward Asselbergs, a Department of Agriculture researcher in Ottawa, invented dried potato flakes, what we more commonly know as instant potatoes, in 1962.

- In 1996, a Saskatoon veterinarian named Dr. Deborah Haines developed a colostrum replacement called HEADSTART. The product, which mimics the first milk produced by a lactating mother and is rich in antibodies, is given to newborn calves to help them digest their first food.

Business

If Canada became a country where reasonable profits could be made safely and honestly, industry and enterprise would flourish and tax revenues would increase as unemployment declined.

–Peter Worthington (1927–), journalist

JUST ABOUT EVERY one of us has popped into a Zellers now and again. It's a great place to do your back-to-school shopping, to pick up a few household items or even to shop for cloth. And almost anyone with a cellphone has heard of Rogers Communications Inc. Elizabeth Arden is a popular name among perfume lovers. Coles The Book People have provided Canadians with reading material for many generations, and folks working in the business sector don't need to be told Grand & Toy makes office supplies, not toys. And who hasn't heard of Bick's Pickles.

For the libation connoisseurs among us, there's Labatt, Jackson-Triggs Vintners, Molson's Brewery, Sleeman's Brewery and Hiram Walker & Sons Limited—all pretty much household names for folks who enjoy entertaining. If you're a movie buff, you've certainly heard of Warner Brothers.

What most of us aren't aware of is that all these businesses, and many other equally recognizable household names, are as Canadian in their roots as Tim Hortons. This chapter chronicles some of these stories, shedding a little light on what it took for these companies to make it in this relatively new country we call home. It also provides a little information on the milestones of some of Canada's longstanding businesses.

First Distillery

If we average out the amount of alcohol consumed in 2006, every Canadian aged 15 and older would have drunk an average of 7.02 litres of distilled spirits. The year before, the Canadian market of the industry alone contributed $935.5 million to the country's economy, and in 2006 vodka was Canadians' favourite hard liquor.

The first distillery in Canada was believed to be built by Jean Talon. In 1668 he set out to build a brewery in what was then New France, but rumour was that it also contained a still. At the time, rum imported from the West Indies was readily available and fairly inexpensive, so there wasn't much call for locals to build the industry in their area. In this regard, Talon's efforts can be considered the equivalent of today's cottage industries. However, by 1769 things changed. That's when the first, official distillery in Canada to make rum from imported molasses was established in Québec City.

Hiram Walker was perhaps the first distiller to set up operations and continue in the business. In 1856 he purchased a plot of land near Windsor, Ontario, and re-established his whiskey business from Detroit, Michigan, to Canada. In just 12 years he built his distillery into the biggest of its kind in Canada. In 1890 Canadian Club whiskey was born, a product that far outlived its creator, selling in more than 150 countries. Although he remained an American citizen, Walker spent most of his years in Canada. The Ontario community of Walkerville bears his name.

Libation Firsts

- Canada's oldest brewery was founded in Montréal, along the St. Lawrence River, in 1786, just four years after 18-year-old John Molson stepped off the boat and onto Canadian soil. Molson immigrated to this country from Lincolnshire, England. Before setting up his own brewery, he worked at another, small operation owned by Thomas Lloyd. Molson spent four years working alongside the more experienced Lloyd before purchasing the business from his superior and starting his own enterprise.

- John H. Sleeman's quality brew has been satisfying Canadians since 1834, but the entrepreneur's first official brewery was established in Guelph, Ontario, in 1851. Business came to a standstill in 1933 during Prohibition, and it wasn't until 1988 that it was revived again, this time by John's great-great grandson, John W. Sleeman.

- Talk about being built for one purpose and being used for an altogether different one—or two! The Tunnels of Moose Jaw were originally built in the late 1800s as an easy way for city employees to maintain the heating systems of downtown buildings. From there, the intricate system of tunnels became a hideaway for poorly treated Chinese immigrants, and by 1920, that hideout doubled as a place for Al Capone to escape authorities fast on his tail for the American gangster's rumrunning during Prohibition. As far as infamous Prohibition-era gangster hideouts go, the Tunnels of Moose Jaw were likely a first for our country.

- Did you know that Canada has an official royal whiskey? A distillery located in Gimli, Manitoba, not far from the shores of Lake Winnipeg, fine-tuned its already smooth whiskey and developed a special blend for the royal visit of King George VI and Queen Elizabeth in 1939. And so it was that Crown Royal, Canada's first and to date only royal whiskey, was formed. It was not only an instant hit with consumers, but it also rightfully pleased the visiting couple.

- Jackson-Triggs is a familiar name to wine lovers, but you may be surprised to know that owners Don Triggs and Allan Jackson didn't start the company until 1989. That's when the pair bought out Labatt's winery division. Since then the company has continued to win awards for their new wines and even wow American wine critics.

- John Labatt Limited, the headquarters for the much-loved Canadian brew, was first established along the Thames River near London, Ontario, in 1847. That's when John Labatt and Samuel Eccles bought out a small brewery started by John Balkwell almost 20 years earlier, in 1828. Labatt made history as one of the few Canadian breweries to survive Prohibition. They accomplished this feat by producing two products containing less than two percent alcohol, which were marketed as "temperance ales." And throughout Prohibition the brewery continued shipping beer to the U.S. The company has gone through a lot of changes over the years, but two things have remained the same: they maintain their commitment to making quality beer, and the present brewery is located in the same area as the original.

First Cosmetic Queen

One of America's wealthiest businesswomen had her beginnings on Canadian soil. Elizabeth Arden was born Florence Nightingale Graham in Woodbridge, Ontario, on December 31, 1878. Following her namesake, Florence tried nursing but found it wasn't to her liking. She waded through a few other jobs, eventually landing a position with E.R. Squibb Pharmaceuticals Company in New York City. That's where she first became interested in skin care, eventually doing her own research in the company's laboratory.

The doors started opening to her profitable future after she worked as a "treatment girl" in a beauty shop, where she linked up with another aspiring entrepreneur, Elizabeth Hubbard. The two women opened a shop of their own on Fifth Avenue, but when their partnership dissolved, Florence took over the business. She changed her name to Elizabeth Arden—using the first name of her former partner, and the last name, Arden, from the Tennyson poem "Enoch Arden." It was at this time that she came up with the idea of her signature red door symbol and started developing tinted powders and rouges.

Eventually, Arden hooked up with a chemist named A. Fabian Swanson, and they began concocting a variety of skin creams and tonics. As the cosmetic line grew, so did her popularity. So much so that a popular saying in the 1930s was: "There are only three American names that are known in every corner of the globe: Singer sewing machines, Coca-Cola and Elizabeth Arden."

Just remember, she was a Canadian first.

Canada's First Coffee King

In my neck of the woods, the idea of a drive-by window at a Tim Hortons donut shop being a fast-food option is laughable. Cars are usually lined up more than a dozen deep, and no sooner have you grabbed your purchase from the window clerk than another car has joined the fold. In this country, Tim Hortons is an addiction among a fair chunk of the population. Most of us enjoy a donut or two now and again, but it's the coffee that keeps people coming back.

The first Tim Horton shop (the shop name was originally singular) welcomed its first customers in 1964 in Hamilton, Ontario. Founded by the NHL player of the same name, the company did well for itself but grew considerably with the marketing talents of Ron Joyce, a former Hamilton police officer who joined the business in 1965. By 1967, after Joyce had already opened two more stores, the two men became full partners. Horton maintained involvement in the business but also continued playing hockey until he died in a car accident in 1974. That's when Joyce purchased Tim's share and took over as sole owner. By then there was already a thriving chain of 40 stores, but by 1990s the corporation went public, and in 1991 multiplied to such an extent that the company welcomed its 500th store, opened in Aylmer, Québec.

As the business increased its number of stores, it also expanded its menu items. Although the stores started off selling coffee and donuts, highlighting the apple fritter and Dutchie, its two original creations, it wasn't long before pies, cakes, soups and sandwiches were added. The company's first attempt at diversity was with the introduction of the Timbit—made from the bite-sized, rounded centre of every donut—in 1976. The idea was gobbled up, as were other additions to the menu. Tim Hortons coffee options also grew with the introduction of flavoured cappuccinos in 1997, and continued with additional varieties.

Perhaps the key to Tim Hortons success is its willingness to change and adapt to change. One of those big changes was the merger of Tim Hortons with Wendy's Restaurants. Daniel P. Murphy, a businessman who owned all the Tim Hortons and Wendy's Restaurant outlets on Prince Edward Island, was the first to come up with idea of merging the two businesses. The first joined store was opened in 1992 in the community of Montague. The experiment was such a success that on August 8, 1995, Wendy's International Inc. merged with TDL Group Ltd., Tim Hortons corporate entity. That merger left Joyce with more of Wendy's shares than its founder, Dave Thomas.

Today, Tim Hortons continues to be one of Canada's most prolific business success stories. As Pierre Berton once wrote, "In so many ways the story of Tim Hortons is the essential Canadian story. It is a story of success and tragedy, of big dreams and small towns, of old-fashioned values and tough-fisted business, of hard work and hockey."

First Pickle Companies

Can you imagine Thanksgiving or Christmas or even a summer picnic without pickles? Although they've been around forever—they're even mentioned in the Bible—the commercial-made products have given us a chance to enjoy the crisp crunch without all that time and energy required to make them. Canada boasts two prime pickle princes: Bick's Pickles and Strub's Pickles. Strub's came along first, founded by Hamilton, Ontario residents Michael and Sophie Strub in 1929. Their product started out as a home-based business as Sophie concocted a huge batch of her homemade pickles to trade for groceries at the local store. When she couldn't keep up with the demand, the family knew they stumbled on the answer to their financial woes. They started making pickles full time, and by the early 1940s Strub Brothers Limited was founded. They remain the largest family-owned pickle manufacturer in the country.

Bick's Pickles had its humble beginnings in 1944 when Jenny and Walter Bick were working around the clock at their southern Ontario farm, trying to use up all of that year's cucumber harvest before they all rotted in the fields. By 1952 they officially entered the retail business, moving their efforts from providing butcher and grocery shops with barrels full of pickles in brine to individually packaged jars of pickles. From there they expanded their product line to include sweet pickles, hot pickles, relishes and much more. The company sold to Robin Hood Flour Mills in 1966, and today is owned by International Multifoods of Wayzata, Minneapolis.

Other Business Firsts

- Everyone knows the Hudson's Bay Company has a long, distinguished business track record, but were you aware it's considered the "oldest, continuously operating company" on the continent? This retail first was established on May 2, 1670.

- In 1854, John Redpath opened Canada's first sugar refinery in Montréal, along the shores of the St. Lawrence River. That original refinery remained open until 1980.

- Theodor Heintzman came to Canada from his native Germany in 1860, but by then he was a well-skilled piano craftsman. He made his first piano on Canadian soil in 1860 and set up Heintzman and Company six years later. Although not everyone bought what he crafted, his impeccable attention to detail earned him no end of accolades, and pianists everywhere knew the name of Heintzman Pianos. By 1890, "the firm was one of Toronto's largest manufacturing firms and was producing one thousand pianos annually." The company continued in business until the mid-1980s.

- Timothy Eaton began his retail empire in 1869. He was the first retailer to offer a money-back guarantee on his merchandise. He spent $6500 to buy a dry goods store on Toronto's Yonge Street. By then Eaton had several years experience in retail, having taken a job in the business on his arrival in Canada in 1854, so it's no surprise that by 1883 he needed to move to a larger venue. He also introduced the Santa Claus Parade to Toronto and was one of the first retailers to offer a catalogue, with the launching of The Wishing Book in 1884.

- Canada's first step into Hollywood, at least when it comes to directing and producing movies, was made by

Louis B. Mayer. Although he wasn't born in Canada, he lived in this country from the age of three until he turned 19, in 1904, and moved to Boston, Massachusetts. He bought the "Gem Theatre" in Haverhill, Massachusetts, and re-opened it as the "Orpheum" in 1907. From there it wasn't long before Mayer was one of the "M"s in MGM. Mayer helped co-found the Hollywood film studio Metro-Goldwyn-Mayer in 1924.

- To say Warner Brothers was a Canadian business venture may be a bit of a stretch, but we can claim a little bit of the Hollywood glory. Jack Warner, founder of the film empire, was born Itzhak Eichelbaum in London, Ontario, in 1892. At the age of two, Jack moved with his family to Youngstown, Ohio. Nevertheless, in 1960 he was honoured with the Order of the British Empire. He was also proud of his Canadian roots, often stating that he was born in Canada. Jack and his brothers started their illustrious career by opening a theatre in Pennsylvania.

- If there ever was an unlikely business hero, those who knew the young K.C. Irving may have pointed in his direction. Born in Bouctouche, New Brunswick, on March 14, 1899, K.C. was considered a bit of a tough kid and was often in tussles in the schoolyard. But by 1924, he'd already served a stint in the Royal Flying Corps, started selling cars and founded Irving Oil— Canada's first family-run oil empire. Initially, Irving Oil was a small chain of gas stations, but it wasn't long before it turned into the biggest petroleum retailer from Québec to New England. In time Irving took over his father's sawmill, J.D. Irving Limited, and continued to expand it until it stretched into Maine, and he is now considered one of the "largest foreign land owners in the U.S." Today, the Irving Group of Companies includes a large contingency of the Atlantic media outlets, aircraft interests and "more ships than the Canadian navy." Because the company is family owned and operated, no one really knows how much it's worth, but some business magazines have pegged it at about $5 billion.

- Canada has its fair share of department stores to be proud of. Woodwards, for example, started out when Charles Woodward opened a small general store on Manitoulin Island in 1877. The business grew into a retail empire, but not without its roadblocks. Woodward almost went bankrupt after one of his managers ran up a huge debt. And in 1890 the first store burned to the ground. But by March 1, 1892, he opened a store on Vancouver's Westminster Avenue and in 1986 Woodward's "26 department stores and 33 discount stores" posted a collective annual sales figure of $1.1 billion. Woodward's sold to the Hudson's Bay Company in 1993.

- You might be surprised to learn that not only is Reitmans a company with Canadian origins, but it also had its beginnings in the early 1900s. Romanian immigrants Herman and Sarah Reitman first used their skills at sewing when they opened American Ladies Tailoring and Dressmaking Company in Montréal. By 1914 they pulled out of the clothing business in favour of operating a general store that they ran until 1926, at which time their four sons joined in the business. At that point the family, once again, looked at rebranding themselves, focusing solely on women's wear. Simply called Reitmans, the store was a success. Within three years the family had opened four stores in Montréal, and in 1936 the chain was expanding to other Canadian cities. Today, the company includes 362 Reitmans stores, about 159 Smart Set stores, and an assortment of Thyme Maternity Penningtons, Addition Elle and other clothing outlets. The Reitman family is still very much involved in the company with Jeremy H. Reitman holding the position of president.

- Canada is certainly a country with an abundant supply of rags-to-riches stories. Such is the scenario behind the weekly magazine, *Maclean's*. The current events and pop-culture magazine was founded in 1905 by John Bayne Maclean, an education major turned journalist. Maclean had already started a magazine called the *Canadian Grocer* in 1887, along with an impressive array of other trade magazines, and had fared well enough to try to expand his corner of the media market. Other notable publications founded by Maclean were *The Financial Post*, in January 1907 and *Chatelaine* in 1928.

- Leon's didn't originally start out as a furniture store. Founded in 1909 by Alban Leon, the A. Leon Company in Welland, Ontario, was initially a dry-goods business. Leon's merchandise expanded until he found himself, without actually planning to, in the furniture business. By 1942, the year Alban passed away, the original store had expanded to accommodate a wide array of household furniture. In 1973, the company opened a 150,000-square-foot retail showroom, and in the process became the country's first example of "big box retailing."

- If you were born before, say, 1998, take a walk down memory lane and try to remember the sights and sounds of a hot summer day. There were birds, I'm sure, the odd breeze, and maybe a distant ringing of a bell that got louder and louder until you recognized the sound and ran into the house begging for change. That sound was the Dickie Dee Ice Cream vendor pedalling his bike up and down city streets selling cool treats to eager youngsters. Dickie Dee Ice Cream was actually Canada's "national ice cream vending company" from 1959 to

2002. Along with its bicycle fleet, the company operated ice cream trucks in select locations. The company,
which was originally founded by Sam Dvorchak in
1951, was sold to the Barish family of Winnipeg in
1959. Under their ownership the company expanded
and diversified, adding more and more products, until
they became one of the "largest ice cream vending
companies in North America." Unilever Canada Inc.
purchased Dickie Dee in 1992.

- Albert Edward LePage started selling real estate in
Toronto in 1913 at the age of 26. But from the beginning he set himself apart from other agents. He came
to work wearing a bow tie and straw hat and became
the first agent in the country to work the job full time.
He claimed to be the first agent to place descriptive
advertisements in newspapers. He was also one of the
first agents to tour sale houses with clients. He used all
this ingenuity in establishing Royal LePage Real Estate
Ltd. shortly after he started selling houses, and the
business never really faltered. Albert died in 1968, but
his company continues to grow and thrive.

- Another thriving Canadian company that knew how
to market itself was Macleods True Value. The store
began as Macleods Limited in Winnipeg, selling largely
farm-related items using the slogan "Factory to Farm."
Roland Macleod came up with the idea for the new
business in 1917 after noticing that farmers of the day
paid far too much for farm supplies. Today the company is owned by Tru*Serv Canada Co-operative Inc.,
labels itself the "nation's largest wholesale hardware
cooperative" and is 100 percent Canadian owned.

- Do you remember shopping for school supplies with
your parents and loading the cart with a dozen or so
Hilroy scribblers? Bet you didn't know the man
behind that product was a Canadian. Roy Hill founded

Canadian Pad and Paper, a business that sold office and school supplies in downtown Toronto in 1918. The company didn't become Hilroy Envelopes and Stationery Limited until 1958 when Hill merged his company with two other companies. In 1994 it was bought out by The Mead Corporation of Dayton, Ohio.

- The East might lay claim to the Irving legacy, but the West isn't without its mega-businessmen. Jimmy Pattison was born in Luseland, Saskatchewan, in 1928, and by the age of seven was pedalling vegetable seeds in Vancouver, where his family had moved. It was his first of many business ventures and, today, the Jim Pattison Group makes a buyout in a game of Monopoly look like petty cash. His company owns media outlets, magazines, car dealerships, the food outlets Overwaitea and Save-On-Foods and communications companies—he even owns the Ripley's Believe it or Not museum, theatre and aquarium...believe it or not.

- Remember the Tilley hat? Yes, that too was a Canadian innovation. Designed by Alex Tilley in 1980, what started out as the design for a hat that wouldn't blow away while you were sailing, has grown into a full line of comfortable sailing clothes.

- The Zellers store is still a mainstay in towns and cities across this country. Zellers Limited was founded on July 13, 1931, after its owner, Walter P. Zeller, purchased 14 American-run Schulte-United stores. Those retail outlets got a facelift, beginning with the erection of new Zellers signs and re-opened for business in 1932 with the motto "Retailers to Thrifty Canadians." The first Zellers store to open was in London, Ontario. The Hudson's Bay Company purchased Zellers in 1981.

- Pet owners will have likely heard of the name Dr Ballard's. William G. Ballard, a Vancouver-area veterinarian who felt strongly about providing healthy food for family pets, started developing his popular line of pet food in the 1920s. Family pets were usually fed table scraps, and it wasn't until the mid to late 1800s that special food was processed for them. By 1931, however, Ballard decided his clients were so thrilled at the results of feeding their pets healthy foods that he devoted himself to full-scale production, opened a small plant and began selling Dr. Ballard's Animal Food Products Limited in earnest. By the time the company sold out to Standard Brands (Canada) Ltd. in 1955, Dr. Ballard's was being sold from coast to coast. Production of Dr. Ballard's products ceased in 2001.

• We all know Coles as a bookstore, but did you know it once sold sporting goods and toys as well? Carl was 22, and his brother, Jack, just 15 when the Colofsky brothers opened their first bookstore in 1935. The brothers opened the bookstore in Toronto because they perceived a need, and Carl needed money for university. At first they called their store The Book Exchange, but in 1938 they changed the name to Coles and a year later opened a second store, this time on the corner of Yonge and Charles Streets. Over the years the business continued to grow and the brothers opened other stores. Although Coles was the first store in Canada to sell the Hula Hoop, the Slinky and the Mechano set, the brothers eventually focused solely on books. The company introduced Coles Notes in 1948, and in 1980, they were one of the first to open a "book superstore" with the "67,000-square-foot World's Biggest Bookstore in downtown Toronto." In 1972 Coles went public, but the brothers maintained control until they finally sold out in 1978. In April 1995, Coles, which was by then owned by Pathfinder Capital, and Smith-Books, formed Chapters Inc.

- Charbroiled burgers were first made popular in Canada after Toronto-area restaurateur Rick Mauran opened the first Harvey's store in 1959. Aside from being a favourite stop when it's dad's turn to cook, Harvey's clocked a Canadian fast food first when it opened the country's first drive-thru restaurant in Pembroke, Ontario.

Crime and Punishment

The purpose of law is to turn passion to reason.

–F.R. Scott (1899–1985), poet

WE CANADIANS THINK of ourselves as polite and easygoing, civilized even. Our communities are safe to walk most times of the day. Should anyone have car trouble and find themselves stalled alongside just about any roadway in the country, someone is apt to stop and ask if they need help. And I actually know people (all right, I admit to doing this myself) who when they find a $20 bill laying on the ground will take it to their local authorities in case the person who lost it comes looking for it.

Of course, that doesn't mean we don't have to lock our doors at night. In 2005, Statistics Canada reported about 2.5 million crimes in the country. The majority, 48 percent, were property crimes, and 12 percent were violent in nature. But if you look back to 1991, when crime rates in this country were at an all-time high, "the national crime rate has decreased by about 30 percent"—our hard-working law enforcement officials would like to hope this is the result of strong deterrents and educational campaigns.

Regardless, wherever people gather, there will be greed, envy, lust and the desire for power. These same human emotions are apt to be the lure that leads some into a life of criminal activity, and they are the reason why we rely on that "strong arm of the law" to keep order in the land.

First System of Corrections

The system of law enforcement when Canada was in its infancy was based on the Old Testament philosophy of an eye for an eye and a tooth for a tooth. If you were caught breaking the law, you knew the punishment would be severe. Depending on the crime, offenders could be shackled into wooden frames called pillories where their head and arms were secured, and they were forced to stand, in public, for days on end. Other modes of punishment included whipping, flogging or even branding the offender with hot metal. Some criminals were banished from the country, though how anyone would know if they snuck back over the border is a bit of a mystery.

Kingston Penitentiary, originally known as the "Provincial Penitentiary of Upper Canada," was built in Kingston, Ontario, between 1833 and 1834, and received its first six inmates on June 1, 1835. Often called "Canada's Big House," Kingston Penitentiary was the country's first federal penitentiary. Several other penitentiaries were built after this one in Kingston, and at the same time asylums also popped up across the country.

The first asylum to open its doors was Rockwood Hospital, built in 1865 next to the Kingston Penitentiary. At the time, prison staff estimated as much as 25 percent of Kingston's prison population was insane, and so a lot of the inmates were transferred to Rockwood. The psychiatrists of the day thought that was a minimalist view, and that all criminals were insane and prisons should be psychiatric hospitals that focused on healing rather than institutions doling out punishment. However, that didn't mean the individuals who were confined to an asylum actually received any kind of treatment.

A movement to reform Canada's prison system began in the early 1920s with the Biggar-Nickle-Draper Committee.

Appointed by the Minister of Justice, Charles J. Doherty,
it was the committee's job to appraise Canada's system of
corrections and suggest changes. In particular, they were
supposed to access procedures surrounding discipline,
education and rehabilitation. In their final report, they
criticized the penal system and pushed for the complete
elimination of any "idea of vengeance not on humanitar-
ian grounds, or because of its painful consequences to the
individual, but solely because of its stupidity and on
grounds of common sense." Instead, the committee urged
the system to work toward preparing inmates to re-enter
society with a renewed commitment to live a good and
productive life.

However, changes to Canada's penal system didn't
occur for a number of years after the committee's recom-
mendations. The Great Depression left a significant portion of Canada's working population without jobs and, as
a result, the crime rate rose. Any idea of prison reform
was put on hold for a time until the economic climate
settled. Other committees were struck, including a 1936
Royal Commission, but reconstructing of any kind took
a backburner until the end of World War II.

Penal System Firsts

- Kingston, Ontario, was home to Canada's first prison for women. In 1835 the first three women—Susan Turner, Hannah Downes and Hannah Baglen—were incarcerated there, amid the male population, after being charged with larceny. It wasn't until 1839 that Kingston formally organized the North Wing of the prison specifically for women.

- Although society generally looked at criminals with contempt, some organizations did include it in their mandate to show mercy to the incarcerated. One of the first two was the Salvation Army, which had worked in Canada's prison system since 1882. The John Howard Society was active even before that. In 1867 a group of concerned church members in Toronto decided spiritual help was needed in their local jail. By 1874 the group was operating as the Prisoners Aid Association of Toronto, and the name didn't change to the John Howard Society until 1931. That's when Reverend J. Dinnage Hobden formed another prison care group in BC and named it the John Howard Society, after the prison reformer of the 1700s.

- Under the leadership of Prime Minister Alexander Mackenzie, the Supreme Court of Canada was officially created on April 8, 1875. Provisions for the formation of the Supreme Court of Canada, the highest court in the country, were outlined in the BNA Act in 1867, but it wasn't made a reality until 1875.

- The first female police magistrate in Alberta, and in the British Empire, was Emily Murphy. She took the position in 1916 after being approached by the Local Council of Women who were concerned that sensitive legal cases regarding women were being discussed and decided on by men.

- It wasn't until 1934 that incarcerated women had their own prison. The Prison for Women was also located in Kingston and built by the male inmates of Kingston Penitentiary. It cost $374,000 to complete and was the only federal prison for women in the country, and all "federally-sentenced women, regardless of their security classification" had to serve their sentences there. The Prison for Women was officially closed in 2000.

- The first Canadian branch of the Elizabeth Fry Society, a group that works with women in the justice system, was founded in 1939 by Agnes Campbell Macphail.

- Punishments doled out for breaking the rules in prison were equally harsh for men and women. Flogging was the least of their concerns. Errant prisoners could be forced to stand in a "coffin-like container with air holes...submerged in ice water [or] put in a dark cell or fed only bread and water." The kind of corporal punishment issued changed over the years, but it wasn't until 1972 that any kind of corporal punishment was abolished.

- Canada's National Parole Board was founded in 1959.

- Bora Laskin was the country's first Jewish Supreme Court jurist and the first Supreme Court Justice. Prime Minister Pierre Trudeau appointed him to the Supreme Court on March 18, 1970, and then Chief Justice on December 27, 1973.

- Programs specifically designed for the social and cultural needs of Aboriginal prisoners were first established in 1972.

- The Office of the Correctional Investigator, founded so that an objective body could investigate inmate complaints, was established on June 7, 1973.

- Young offenders in the penal system required special consideration, and in 1984 the Young Offenders Act was passed to address those needs.

- The first correctional institution geared to the concerns of Aboriginal people was the Okimaw Ohci Healing Lodge. It was built in Maple Creek, Saskatchewan, and opened its doors to female Aboriginal offenders in 1995. Aboriginal men were first housed in a facility geared to their specific social and cultural needs in 1996 with the opening of the Pe Sakastew Centre in Hobbema, Alberta.

First Police Presence

The first official police force in the country started out with a handful of officers assigned to the Dominion Police. Formed in 1868, the constables serving in this peacekeeping venture were charged with protecting Parliament Hill and its many government buildings. By 1911, that role had expanded, and members of the Dominion Police force were assigned to keep order throughout the eastern portion of this large country.

After Confederation in 1867, when the entire country came under the control of the Dominion of Canada, Sir John A. Macdonald set about to establish some semblance of order in the west. In June 1874 the North West Mounted Police (NWMP) was established, and the first group of about 400 officers was recruited, trained and dispatched from what is now Winnipeg to new settlements farther west. Their first official outpost was at Fort Whoop-Up—a settlement along southern Alberta's Old Man River with a reputation for excessive whiskey drinking and revelry.

Meanwhile, things took a little longer to organize in the wilds of Canada's north, but with rumblings of the discovery of gold deposits and the promise of getting rich quick, the area experienced a population boom and with it, the need for someone to keep the peace. On June 1, 1895, a newly developed contingency of the NWMP left Regina to set up its first detachment in the Yukon.

Domestic order wasn't the only contribution of the NWMP. From 1899 to 1902 the police force served England in the South Africa War, and their efforts were recognized officially in 1904 when King Edward VII added "Royal" to their name. Members worked to enforce the War Measure's Act during World War I, and in May 1919, the force was again called upon in a special capacity to bring order to a turbulent Winnipeg during its General Strike.

At this point in history it was clear a national police force was essential in maintaining consistent order throughout the country. On February 1, 1920, the Royal North West Mounted Police and the Dominion Police Force merged to form the Royal Canadian Mounted Police (RCMP). The force was headquartered in Ottawa and members stationed in all communities across the country.

Other RCMP Firsts

- The RCMP opened its first Crime Detection Lab in 1937.

- The first female constables to serve in the force—32 of them—were admitted to a Regina RCMP depot for training on September 18 and 19, 1974. All 32 members of Troop 17 graduated on March 3, 1975.

- Oddly enough, a woman's uniform was at first quite different from the high boots and breeches the men wore. Initially, the women donned their red serge over a skirt and high heels. They even carried an official hand clutch! They didn't start wearing the same uniform as their male counterparts until 1999.

- Dog sleds were the typical method of transportation for RCMP members in the Yukon, and the last dog sled patrol retired in 1969.

First Couple to be Hanged

In the early days of settlement, Canada must have seemed the land of promise. A vast expanse, most of which had yet to be explored, was overflowing with trees and vegetation of all kinds. Rivers and streams flowed thick with fish. Large populations of moose and deer and other wildlife meant anyone with two legs and half a heart shouldn't starve. For new immigrants to this country, many who'd left behind rather difficult circumstances in their homeland, Canada offered the hope for a better future.

That was certainly the case for the family of a young Mary O'Brien. Natives of Ireland, her family believed her future would be more promising than life with them, and so at the tender age of 12 years Mary was sent her to live with a sister in Connecticut.

In 1855 Mary married Richard Aylward, and the couple road the wagon train north from New York to Hastings County, Ontario, where they settled down with their three young daughters in 1861. Neighbours gathered together to help them build their log house, based on the government regulations of the day, and all seemed good for a time. Then on May 16, 1862, Mr. Munro, a neighbour of the Alywards, noticed one of his hens was missing. He brought it to the attention of his wife, who said she remembered hearing the sound of gunfire. Since their chickens had developed the habit of wandering over to the Aylwards' wheat fields for dinner, the Munros arrived at the conclusion that their neighbour Richard was up to no good. Accompanied by his son Alexander, the senior Munro was quick to confront the young man.

Richard denied any allegations that he'd shot one of the Munros' chickens, and the trio took a walk into the field to prove the point. As they say, things went from bad to worse. An altercation took place and Aylward and Munro tussled over a gun. Munro ended up with 29 lead pellets to his backside, at which point a flustered and panicked Mary arrived at the scene armed with a scythe. Lashing out to, in her words, "protect her husband," Mary inflicted several wounds to Munro, one to his arm and another to his neck. When word got out about the attack, the couple was arrested. Munro, injured though he was, refused to be cared for by an "Indian doctor" and died a week later.

A lawyer today would have a heyday with this case, ripping it apart to defend the young couple. Richard hadn't inflicted any life-threatening injuries, and Mary insisted she acted only to defend her husband. With medical attention, Munro would have likely survived the ordeal. Incredibly, though, the Aylwards were found guilty of murder and sentenced to death. At 11:15 AM on December 10, 1862, the couple was hanged side by side, leaving their three daughters to be raised by strangers.

Other Capital Punishment Firsts

- In 1859, if you were convicted of anything from rape to murder to "casting away a ship and exhibiting a false signal endangering a ship," you'd be sentenced to death.

- The Department of Justice lists the first "official" execution as that of Modiste Villebrun. He was put to death on May 3, 1867, for killing his wife and his lover's husband.

- In 1869, capital offences were reduced to murder, rape and treason.

- The first woman hanged on her own was Phoebe Campbell. She met her maker at the end of a rope on July 15, 1871, after being found guilty of murdering her husband. Before her execution, she wrote a confession, telling of the abuse she suffered at his hands.

- Canada's first "professional executioner" whose services were paid for by the federal government was John Radclive. He exercised his professional services from 1892 to his death in 1911.

- The job of Canada's official hangman wasn't vacant for long. When John Radclive died in 1911, his assistant, Arthur Bartholomew English, took over the position in 1912. At some point he assumed the pseudonym of Arthur Ellis, which some sources suggest was in recognition of the British executioner John Ellis. Either way, the Canadian Ellis executed his job (no pun intended) enthusiastically until March 28, 1935, when a hanging went horribly wrong. The criminal in question was one Thomasina Sarao. Thomasina and her two accomplices were sentenced to death after being found guilty of a murder and insurance fraud. Ellis made his way to the Montréal's women's jail prepared to weigh Thomasina in order to determine the length of rope required to break her neck. But his request was denied, and he based his calculations on what turned out to be incorrect information. The weight he was given was under by more than 14 kilograms. The weight differential, combined with the longer length of rope used, resulted in the poor Thomasina losing her head—quite literally. It was the first and last time a woman in Canada was decapitated during a hanging.

- The only method of capital punishment sanctioned by Canada's federal government was hanging, a decision believed to be based on the country's British and French ancestry and the practice of capital punishment in those countries.

- Twenty-nine year old Ronald Turpin and Arthur Lucas, 54, both found guilty of murder, were the last people hanged in this country. They died in Toronto's Don Jail on December 10, 1962.

- Capital punishment was abolished in Canada on July 14, 1976.

- The first rumblings pushing for the death penalty's reinstatement were officially brought forward in the House of Commons in 1987.

Other Law and Order Firsts

- Alex Decoteau earned a position on the Edmonton Police Department as the first full-blooded Aboriginal to join a Canadian municipal police force. He topped that achievement by becoming one of Edmonton's first motorcycle police officers. But Decoteau first made headlines on June 29, 1909, after he nailed a five-mile run, setting a new Western Canadian record with a time of 27.45.2. He continued to rack up accolades with four first-place finishes in the Alberta Provincial Championships in Lethbridge in 1910, and earned a spot in the 1912 Olympics in Sweden—the only athlete from Saskatchewan and Alberta to do so. Alex Decoteau was inducted into the Alberta Sports Hall of Fame, and in 1916 joined the 200th Sportsman Battalion with the goal of bringing his swiftness to the war front. He transferred to the 49th Edmonton Regiment and, on October 30, 1917, was shot dead by a sniper's bullet. He was just 30 years old.

- Wayne Clifford Boden was convicted of raping and killing at least three women between July 23, 1968, and 1971. Nicknamed the "vampire rapist" because he left bite marks on his victims' breasts, he was the first person in North America convicted as a result of forensic odontological evidence.

- In 1989, Yvonne Johnson became the first Canadian woman found guilty of first-degree murder. Johnson was originally facing life in jail with "no chance of parole for 25 years," but was granted day parole on January 31, 2008.

- When Steven Truscott was convicted of the rape and murder of his 12-year-old friend, Lynne Harper, he became the youngest Canadian ever sentenced to the death penalty. After the abolishment of the death penalty, his sentence was commuted to life in prison. He proclaimed his innocence from the beginning, and on August 28, 2007, the Court of Appeal revoked Truscott's earlier guilty conviction.

- *Maclean*'s magazine has been rating the quality of Canadian universities for many years now, but it wasn't until 2007 that it started ranking another type of educational institution—law schools. The first-ever law school ranking was published in September of that year, and according to the magazine, schools were rated not on whether they were the hardest school to get into, but rather the "quality of the output of each school." The first law school to receive the first-place ranking under the category of Common Law Schools was the University of Toronto. The University of Montreal earned the top spot under the category of Civil Law Schools.

All Things Art

*Art is a necessity—an essential part of our enlightenment
process. We cannot, as a civilized society, regard ourselves as
being enlightened without the arts.*

–Ken Danby, Canadian artist (1940–2007)

LONG BEFORE PENS, paper and varieties of paint colours were
available; humankind has attempted to express itself
through art. The oldest example of this is what's left of
the Venus of Tan-Tan. Dating back to sometime between
300,000 and 500,000 BC, the six-centimetre-long Venus
of Tan-Tan is a headless, genderless quartzite sculpture
painted with red ochre. No one really knows its true significance, but clearly its creator desired to say something.

So it's no surprise, then, that long before European
settlers arrived in this country, Native people had established their own masterpieces. An assortment of petro-
glyphs, found in northwestern Ontario, is the oldest
known example of Aboriginal art dating back to 5000 BC.
One of the first known Native carvings dates to around
3000 BC. The sculpture, discovered at Coteau-du-lac in
southwestern Québec, looks like "a human face into the
surface of a rock."

The arrival of Europeans to Canadian soil merely
expanded the repertoire of an already established society
well practiced in exploring itself through the arts. Immigrants from around the world brought with them their
own traditions, and on arriving in their new home developed new ones until what we have today is a truly diverse
mosaic, in every sense of the word.

First Totem Poles

To anyone lucky enough to stand in its presence, a totem pole is simply awe-inspiring. Images carved deep into the flesh of a felled tree trunk whisper tales of another time. They're a concrete reminder of life long ago—it's what totem poles were meant to be.

In the late 1990s, I watched as Aboriginal carver James Madam wielded an axe and long knife to chop away at the trunk of what must have been quite an old tree. With hard, harsh movements, he chipped away chunks of the wood until he'd outlined a grizzly bear, killer whale, beaver, big frog, small frog, a human and the mythical gryphon—the local high school's mascot. The animal symbols represented the Laksilyu, Gilseyhu, Tsayu, Gitdumden and Laksamishu—the five clans of the Wet'suwet'en Nation of northern BC. The gryphon (half eagle and half lion) crowned the top of the pole. From there Madam spent weeks fine-tuning his sculpture, then painting it, and when it was ready, the five clans and an entire high school gathered together to erect it in front of Smithers Senior Secondary School. It was the first totem pole raised in the town since the 1970s, when most of the existing poles were torn down by the non-Native residents. This new pole represented a step in the healing process between the two cultures.

Aboriginal people have used totem poles, in varying frequency from tribe to tribe, to tell the stories and mark milestones in their history. It's a tradition that continues to this day. But when did it begin?

Where to find the oldest totem poles in Canada is often a topic of dispute. Several prime examples of these testaments to another time are found in the village of Kitwancool. Located deep in BC's northern interior, and far off the well-travelled Yellowhead Highway, a couple dozen or so of these towering giants are clustered to one side of the village. Like cemetery tombstones, they're a bleached grey in colour, worn and aged by decades of weather, and if you stand nearby on a windy day you can hear them whisper.

Although there's no definitive time line when these Kitwancool totems were carved, they're thought to be among the oldest on mainland Canada. There are some totem poles, however, that predate even these dinosaurs. You'll need to take a ferry ride from Prince Rupert to the Queen Charlotte Islands and then charter a tour boat to see them, but it will be well worth the effort. These totems are located on Anthony Island, Ninstints, just off the main Queen Charlotte Island. The site, located in Haida territory, is a United Nations World Heritage Site, where 32 poles have survived since, some scientists estimate, the 1840s or so. They're believed to be the "oldest collection in situ (still standing)."

Other Aboriginal Art Firsts

- The Dorset Palaeo-Eskimos lived a fairly insular life in some of Canada's remotest north, around Cape Dorset on Baffin Island as long as 3000 years ago. Although they didn't travel and mingle with other northern dwellers, archaeological evidence suggests their lives were full and varied. Among the artifacts recovered from their villages are typical tools for daily living, but works of art were also found. Along with the soap-stone lamps and bone sled shoes were painted wooden religious masks and ivory miniatures of animals and people.

- The Sechelt image, which dates back sometime between 100 BC and 500 AD, is a mass of stone carved by the Sechelt First Nation, Salish people of coastal British Columbia. The sculpture depicts a full-grown human figure holding a young child. The adult image is of a man's face, a phallus with arms that grab hold of the man and a vulva. Canadian archaeologist and anthropologist Wilson Duff had interpreted the sculpture this way: "His ambiguity is absolute: 'male strength' is also 'mother and child.'"

- John White made the first known paintings of Inuit life in 1576, during his travels with the Frobisher expeditions.

- Some time between 1620 and 1640, the Iroquois first used wampum belts, made from beads fashioned from the quahog Atlantic clam, in Canada. It was around this time that glass beads were sewn onto cloth, instead of the traditional materials of deerskin.

- Although there isn't a lot of documentation on the art of birch bark biting, it is thought to have developed sometime in the 17th century among Native people in the northern parts of Canada's prairie provinces and into the Northwest Territories. Simply put, women would separate the tissue-like sheets from a section of birch bark, fold it into eighths or sixteenths, and use their teeth to bite intricate patterns into the tissue. What resulted was often a lot more complicated than the equivalent of a paper snowflake—eagles, flowers and other scenes were unfolded after they were done. It is considered one of the "oldest aboriginal art forms."

- Although exact dating is difficult, the Canadian Museum of Civilization in Ottawa-Hull claims it has the world's oldest totem pole. The sample was transported to the museum from northern BC (where the oldest collections still stand) and was dated somewhere between 1820 and 1860.

- Although there are differing views of the origin of the jingle dress, it's generally thought to be a tradition that stems from the North American plains Indians, such as the Ojibwa and Chippewa. The dress was worn during powwows, and a woman who donned such a dress was accepting the responsibility of a medicine woman. Originally, the jingle portion of the dresses, which look like little bells hanging in horizontal stripes across the dress, were made of shells, but after European settlers arrived, Native people used the metal from snuff tins and fashioned them into small cones to make the bells.

- What was used to create art throughout history was always dependent on what was available. On either of Canada's coastlines, shells and whalebones were often used in making beads to adorn clothing. Native people living on Canada's plains had no access to those items, but they had other alternatives. Porcupine quills, for example, were used to decorate clothing and footwear and used to create elaborate baskets.

- Another art form that's uniquely Canadian and credited to the Athapaskan peoples living across Canada's
  North and into Alaska is that of moose and caribou
  tufting. Tufting dates back to the 1920s and 1930s.
  Around that time a Métis woman living in the Fort
  Simpson area, named Boniface Lafferte, was watching
  a nun do "punch work." The nun was using wool and
  basically punching small strips of it into a piece of
  cloth in a method similar to rug hooking. Ms. Lafferte
  thought she could use moose hair and do something
  similar, and she created amazing collages of flowers
  and other natural settings, such as butterflies and
  birds, trimmed and dyed a variety of colours and set
  on dark backgrounds. The end result was a soft, three-
  dimensional picture. Hair from the beard of caribou
  and porcupine quills are also often used.

First Theatrical Performance

The tug of exploring the unknown lands of the New World was a hard one to resist. For Marc Lescarbot (1570–1642), even his career as a lawyer and his responsibilities to the parliament of Paris wasn't enough to hold him back when he was offered a chance to travel to the New World. In May 1606 he boarded the *La Rochelle*, a ship bound for Acadia.

Lescarbot's talents went far beyond that of the legal world. Lescarbot was a writer, and as he sailed from France across the Atlantic he chronicled his journey, producing works such as *Histoire de la Nouvelle-France* and *Nova Francia: A Description of Acadia, 1606*, earning him the reputation as being the area's first historian.

But his accomplishments didn't end there. Lescarbot toyed with theatre, and he put his writing talents into action by composing a musical play entitled *Le Theatre de Neptune en la Nouvell-France* (The Theatre of Neptune in New France). It ran for the first time in November 1606. It is widely acclaimed as being the first non-native theatrical production ever held in North America, earning Lescarbot the title of "father of Canadian theatre." And the cast of 11 performed from several boats at the Port adding another theatrical milestone as the "first floating theatrical presentation" in the country.

The Neptune Theatre in Halifax opened in 1962 as a tribute to that first theatrical performance, and productions of Lescarbot's play are held regularly.

Photography Firsts

When it comes to taking photographs, whether they are the still or moving kind, Canadians have had their fair share of firsts in this area. For example, panoramic images are commonplace today, thanks to John R. Connon of Elora, Ontario. Connon's camera was secured to a tripod equipped with a wheel, and the user only had to turn it in a complete circle to capture a full 360-degree picture. It was a great device for taking photographs of large groups or a panorama of a cityscape.

Connon was actually living in New York when he first patented his Cycloramic Panoramic Camera in 1887. He secured patents in England and Canada the next year.

Arthur Williams McCurdy, long time personal secretary for Alexander Graham Bell, had a few ideas for inventions himself. He developed "an apparatus for developing flexible photographic film" and secured a patent for the invention in December 1890. But it wasn't initially marketed in Canada, and in 1903 McCurdy sold his invention to Rochester, New York native George Eastman. A short time later "Kodak Developing Machines" were being sold—a nice addition to his line of Kodak cameras.

While Eastman's development of a roll of film for his Kodak cameras boosted his own business, it also opened the doors to the world of motion pictures—and Canadians have added their own flare to that industry. The first Canadian filmmaker, James Freer, is also credited with making the world's first film advertisement. In 1897, the Manitoba native put together a mini-movie about life on the Prairies, which was used to tempt folks in the United Kingdom into immigrating to Canada.

George and Andrew Holland, brothers from Ottawa who moved to New York City, are credited with hosting the first "motion picture showing in North America" after they opened a Kinetoscope Parlour there in 1894. (A kinetoscope is an early, single-viewing device for watching film.)

In the world of documentaries, Canada scored another first. In 1922, American filmmaker Robert J. Flaherty produced *Nanook of the North*, a silent feature-length film about life in Canada's remote North. The story was based around Nanook, an Inuit hunter who was also a friend of Flaherty's, and although there are parts of the film Flaherty is said to have orchestrated, it was the first time life in the North was filmed in its natural environment without intervention.

Leo-Ernest Ouimet is generally considered by those in the Canadian film industry as "the most important man in the history of Canadian cinema." He had a vision where folks would visit a movie theatre and feel like they were sitting in their own home. Comfortable and plush chairs replaced hard, kitchen chairs, and the overall environment warmed with rich colour tones and sculptured walls. And even though the going rate for a seat at the Nickelodeon in 1907 was just a nickel, he opened The Ouimetoscope in Montréal—the "first deluxe motion picture theatre in the world"—and charged patrons two or three times that amount.

Other Film Firsts

- Canada's first national film producer was Canadian Government Motion Picture Bureau in 1918. The National Film Board (NFB) replaced it in 1939, through the passing of the National Film Act. The National Film Board of Canada is the largest government-run film operation in the world.

- The world's first "government-funded film studio dedicated to women filmmakers" is Studio D. The National Film Board of Canada started Studio D in 1974, in conjunction with International Women's Year, and it continued successful productions until 1996.

- "Picture This…" is the country's first international disability film festival, kicking off its first festival in 2001. The films are about individuals with some sort of disability, or are produced by those individuals, and are held annually. The non-profit event is the brainchild of the Calgary Scope Society.

- Vancouver is the premiere destination for filmmakers in Canada. It often goes by the nickname "Hollywood North."

- Canada's largest media company is the Toronto-based Alliance Atlantis Communications Inc.

- On the international stage, Canada's largest grossing film is the comedy *Porky's*.

First IMAX Theatre

The five-storey high and 22-metre-wide screen known as IMAX (Image Maximum) was the collective brainchild of Graeme Ferguson, Roman Kroitor, Robert Kerr and William C. Shaw. The idea for a super-sized film format came about after Expo '67, which was held in Montréal. The multi-projector system used at that venue provided a large-screen format and a unique viewing experience, but it had a lot of problems. The four Canadians took the idea a step further, used high-resolution, large film stock and projected the images onto an equally large screen. The viewers' entire range of vision was completely covered by the projected images, putting them right in the scene and providing sensory stimulation along with a visual burst. The end result was the IMAX we know today.

IMAX Facts

- The first IMAX showing was at Expo '70 in Osaka, Japan.

- The first IMAX film was the 17-minute-long short film *Tiger Child*. It was directed by Canadian Donald Brittain.

- The IMAX theatre Cinesphere, which opened at Ontario Place in Toronto, was the country's first permanent IMAX theatre.

- The first, permanent 3-D version of IMAX is located in Vancouver.

- *The Old Man and the Sea*, which came out in 1999, was the first "fully-animated film to be released on IMAX screens and win an Oscar."

- The first feature film released into IMAX was *Treasure Planet*.

The Group of Seven

That the wild and rugged landscape of Canadian geography inspired the artistically inclined is no surprise. Susanna Moodie and her sister Catherine Parr Traill wrote of their experiences and impressions immigrating to Canada from England as early as 1832. And writers before them, such as humorist Thomas Chandler Haliburton (1796–1865), brought a smile to early Canadian readers.

The world of visual art was no different. Dutch artist Cornelius Krieghoff, working through the mid-1800s, was among the first to immortalize scenes from early Québec on canvass. Another Canadian artist, Paul Kane, similarly documented scenes in western Canada. But it was undoubtedly the Group of Seven and their affiliates who, for many art aficionados, were the first to put Canada on the map of the art world in a big way.

The first "seven" in the Group of Seven, which was officially formed in 1919, were all painters: Franklin Carmichael, Lawren Harris, A.Y. Jackson, Frank Johnston, Arthur Lismer, J.E.H. MacDonald and Frederick Varley. Two other Canadian artists, Tom Thomson and Emily Carr, were closely affiliated with the group but not official members. Thomson died before he ever had the chance to join—he was the first Canadian artist to die mysteriously after falling from his canoe into the murky waters of Algonquin Park. The circumstances surrounding his death are still unknown. Carr, an eccentric and mysterious but brilliant artist more apt to keep her own company, wrote of how she admired the work of the group members. As a woman in the male-dominated art world, she wasn't taken seriously in her day, but was later recognized as a major influence and Canada's first major female artist. She was also the first woman to travel throughout the First Nations' remote villages of the West

Coast, painting the natural landscape. In 1927 she was invited to take part in a Group of Seven exhibit at the National Gallery of Canada, making this the first time she'd shown her work in such a prestigious venue. Members of the Group of Seven nicknamed her "The Mother of Modern Arts."

To a large extent, it was the members of the Group of Seven who first collectively documented the Canadian landscape so extensively—prior to their efforts, the Canadian landscape was thought a drab and unappealing inspiration. They travelled extensively throughout Ontario, and after their first official exhibition in 1920, were recognized as "pioneers of a new, Canadian, school of art."

As they continued with their work, some members left the group and others joined. Those that remained started expanding their search for new inspiration, travelling west to British Columbia and north to the Arctic—they were the first non-Aboriginal artists to paint the Arctic.

In 1933, the group, which had grown in numbers beyond its first seven members, decided to disband the original group and form a new, larger collective called The Canadian Group.

Canada's First Comic Book Hero

Dreams can come true, and not only is that at least part of the message behind the Action Comics series *Superman*, it was definitely a reality for Toronto-born Joe Shuster and his American counterpart, Jerome Siegel. Joe's family had moved to Cleveland, Ohio, in 1923 when Joe was just nine, but it wasn't until they moved again, this time into Jerry's neighbourhood, that the two attended the same school and worked at the high school paper.

It wasn't long before the two discovered a common interest in fantasy and science fiction and struck up a friendship. And while other youngsters their age were out playing ball or working to raise money to buy a car, Joe and Jerry were busy making a "fanzine." Their first couple of attempts at producing a comic they hoped would gain wide appeal didn't have anything at all to do with the *Superman* theme. Their first creation, *Snoopy and Smiley*, was a comic about a cave man and *The Time Crusaders* dealt with time travel. But by 1933, they'd conceived of what would become the most famous comic-book hero of all time—*Superman*.

The world, or at least the neighbourhood where Joe and Jerry lived, got their first glimpse of the superhuman who's so powerful he combines the strength and characteristics of several mythical heroes, in *The Reign of Superman*. However, the Superman in this first instalment isn't a good guy at all but a villain. But the co-creators weren't entirely happy with this incarnation and decided to make him a hero. They continued on with other adjustments, too. Shuster wasn't satisfied with his drawings and, after ripping them up, put the project aside for a time and went on to another script, *Goober, The Mighty*.

Meanwhile, the pair continued thinking about Super-man, and in 1934, they finally came up with a rendition they agreed upon, both when it came to the artwork and the persona. At this point, Superman had his dual iden-tity, his daytime persona of Clark Kent—named after actors Clark Gable and Kent Taylor. He could also "leap tall buildings in a single bound, was faster than a speed-ing bullet and more powerful than a locomotive." The character of Lois Lane was based on Siegel's love interest who, as it happens, later became his wife.

Action Comics printed the first issue of *Superman* in June 1938. The front cover featured the new super hero hoisting a car over his head as he saves his dear Lois. It was an immediate hit.

Shuster and Siegel sold the rights to DC Comics in 1940.

Canadians continued to have an impact on this cul-tural icon. The first movie version of the comic, produced in 1978 by Warner Brothers, featured Québec-born Glenn Ford as Superman's earthly father and Margo Kidder, a native of Yellowknife, Northwest Territories, as Lois Lane.

Other Art Firsts

- The first record of Europeans experiencing one of the traditional dances of Native people is found in the journals of Jacques Cartier. In 1534, he wrote how "wild men dancing and making many signs of joy and mirth" approached him at Chalem Bay.

- Molly Lamb Bobak was just 20 years old when she enlisted in the Canadian Women's Army Corp in November 1942. It wasn't long before her artistic talents were recognized, and she was appointed as a Canadian war artist. The first woman to be officially named to such a position, Bobak spent considerable time in Holland, putting a face to war's destruction by painting the devastation she found there during World War II.

- If you ask women working in Canada's art scene which female artist stood out in Canada during the 1900s, they would more than likely say Joyce Wieland. A painter who ventured into mixed media and other forms of art, Wieland was considered by many as Canada's best female artist of the 20th century and the country's first feminist artist. In 1971 Wieland held a solo exhibition at the National Gallery of Canada, making her the first "living Canadian woman artist" to do so.

- Lynn Johnston is widely known for her cartoon strip *For Better or Worse*—and that kind of recognizable fame in the world of cartoons isn't an easy feat. In 1985 she was formally recognized for her work, winning the Reuben Award for Outstanding Cartoonist of the Year. It was the first time a woman had won the award, which is distributed by the Cartoonist Society. She clocked another first in 1988 when she became the first female member of that society.

- Edward Poitras was the first Aboriginal artist invited to represent the country at Venice Biennal, a major art exhibition held in Venice, Italy, every odd year. His work graced that event in 1995.

- Florence Wyle (1881–1968) logged a number of firsts for women in the world of sculpture. In 1928 she was one of several founding members of the Sculptor's Society of Canada, and "she was the first woman sculptor to become a member of the Royal Canadian Academy of Arts."

- Before 1967, no one in the world had ever heard of a program that promoted artistic endeavours for prison inmates. But that year, the Prison Arts Foundation of Canada was formed, and in 1972 it was incorporated into a non-profit foundation. Since then hundreds of inmates have taken part in the program, and some— like Pierre Dupuis—have even gone on to study at the university level after serving their time.

Firsts in Literature

If you're a book lover, chances are you've been to a book signing or two in your day. Listening to your favourite author read and getting him or her to sign their book is certainly a thrill. But long distance travel often means jetlag, long line-ups, and added expenses to all involved. With so many book signings under her belt, the experience got author Margaret Atwood thinking. What if writers and publishers could access the electronic media to reach a larger audience with their book readings and still sign their books for their fans? The end result was the LongPen Network, a system developed by Unotchit Inc. in 2006 whereby authors are networked to a variety of bookstores in any number of locations, provide their book readings or question and answer sessions and sign autographs all from the comfort of their homes.

The autographs are signed using an electronic writing tablet, which viewers can see on the video screen where they've watched you share your reading. The writer is also in front of a screen and can see the person he or she is signing their book for. The book (or other item) is placed under the automatic writing pen at the store and the author picks up the magnetic pen on his end to sign. He pushes the "Send" button, and a pen, attached to the instrument on the receiving end, inscribes the book.

First Literary Awards

Canadian writers were recognized officially for the first time with the Governor General's Literary Awards in 1937, when the awards were first instituted. Bertram Brooker was honoured as the first recipient of the award for his novel *Think of The Earth*, published in 1936 by Thomas Nelson & Sons. The 1937 literary award for fiction went to Canada's first female recipient, Laura G. Salverson, for her novel *The Dark Weaver*. Interestingly enough, the following year another woman was so honoured when Gwethalyn Graham received the award for fiction for her book *Swiss Sonata*.

Laura Salverson was also the first woman to receive the Governor General's Award for non-fiction for her book *Confessions of an Immigrant's Daughter*, published in 1939 by Macmillan Co. of Canada. That accomplishment also gave Salverson the distinction of being the first Canadian to win more than one Governor General's Award.

First Ballet Company

Canada's premiere ballet company is also the longest-running ballet company on the continent. The company was originally founded by Gweneth Lloyd and Betty Farrally under the name Winnipeg Ballet Club in 1939 and changed its name to the Winnipeg Ballet in 1941. In 1953 Queen Elizabeth II granted the "Royal" prefix to its name, and the company has dazzled audiences with first-rate performances ever since. It was the first dance company to earn that distinction and remains the only dance company in the country with the Royal prefix.

Members of the Royal Winnipeg Ballet toured for the first time in 1954, and today almost half of every year the performances are taken on the road. The company's most well-known and prima ballerina is Evelyn Hart. She joined the company in 1976 and remained with them until 2005.

First Québec Symphony Orchestra

It was the French who coined the phrase "joie de vivre," and in the French culture that joy of living is evident in everything they do. So it's fitting that the country's first symphony orchestra was formally organized in Québec City, the heart of French Canada.

The Québec Symphony Orchestra wasn't initially started with permanence in mind. Conductor Joseph Vezina led a group of musicians brought together for three performances, from June 23 to 25, 1902, as part of Laval University's jubilee celebrations. The performance earned rave reviews, and three instrumentalists from that original group—Joseph Talbot, Raoul Vezina and Leonidas Dumas—lobbied their colleagues to form a permanent organization. In early October of that same year, the Québec Symphony Orchestra was officially formed with 25 members, under the continued tutelage of conductor Joseph Vezina.

On November 28, 1902, the Québec Symphony gave its first performance as a group. It was a rather short performance, likely designed to whet the appetite of the city's music lovers, but it was followed by a lengthier one on December 3. The symphony hasn't looked back since and was incorporated on March 20, 1906.

On June 3, 1927, the Québec Symphony formally adopted its motto, *Arte alitur fulegatque* (Art nourishes and enlightens). And aside from not holding a single performance from March 1918 to March 1919, because of the tumultuous period at the end of World War I and the onset of the Spanish Flu epidemic, the symphony has been delighting audiences with their particular brand of joie de vivre, making it the oldest and still active symphony in the country.

Here are a few more firsts for Québec's landmark symphony:

- On February 23, 1903, the Québec Symphony saw its first major expansion with the addition of 14 musicians.

- The orchestra demonstrated its commitment to supporting Canadian talent early on when it premiered Joseph Vezina's three comic operas: *Le Laureat, Le Rajah* and *Le Fetiche*.

- Joseph Vezina was the symphony's conductor for 22 years. He died in 1924.

- In 1968, Pierre Dervaus became the symphony's first foreign-born conductor to take on the position of artistic director.

- As with any organization, the more people you get together the more possibility for dissention—and an orchestra is necessarily large. In the fall of 1935, organizational disagreements led to a group of musicians breaking away and forming the Cercle philharmonique de Québec. The group survived for seven years before they once again merged with the Québec Symphony on June 25, 1942.

- The year 1945 marked the first time the symphony added afternoon children's concerts. It also hosted its first young soloists' competition with 13-year-old Janine Lachance announced the competition's first winner.

- The symphony performed for the first time in Toronto in July 1983.

Other Music Firsts

- Canada's first regional orchestra was the Atlantic Symphony Orchestra. The group was established on June 12, 1968, pulling talent from the communities of Halifax and Sydney, Nova Scotia, and the New Brunswick communities of Saint John, Moncton and Fredericton, following the close of the Halifax and New Brunswick symphonies. The orchestra continued to perform until 1983. It remains, to this day, the country's only regional orchestra.

- Although *Oh Canada!* was first performed on June 24, 1880, St. Jean-Baptiste Day, it wasn't officially adopted as the country's national anthem until July 1, 1980.

- In 1970, Anne Murray earned herself an American gold record for the single "Snowbird." It was the first time such an honour was awarded to a Canadian female solo singer.

- Canadian musicians landed themselves in the *Guinness Book of World Records,* on May 15, 2000, after they set a new world record. The Vancouver Symphony Orchestra (VSO), along with 6400 band students from all around BC, gathered to form the world's largest orchestra. VSO director Bramwell Tovey led the nine-minute, 44-second presentation of Beethoven's 9th Symphony (*Ode to Joy*).

- A 33-year-old Saskatchewan woman named Tania Miller became the first woman in the country to lead a major Canadian orchestra when she was appointed music director of the Victoria Symphony in 2003–04.

Games People Play

I sold the memoirs of my sex life to a publisher—they are going to make a board game out of it.

–Woody Allen, (1935–), actor

CANADIANS HAVE A reputation for being a tad stoic. We don't like to ruffle any feathers; we like to keep the peace at all costs—well, some of us do. Although we enjoy having a good time, we'd prefer not to make a big scene. We applaud politely following live performances, but we rarely get carried away and give a standing ovation. Overall I guess you could say we're a controlled bunch—and when you think about it, you'd have to be pretty controlled if there's any truth to Pierre Berton's characterizing of a "true Canadian" as someone "who can make love in a canoe without tipping."

We do know how to have fun, and if some of the amazing games Canadians have invented are any indication, we're pretty good at sharing the lighter side of ourselves. Take a quick tour through the games isle of any Toys R Us and you may be surprised at how many Canadian-inspired games you'll come across. Trivia buffs surely know Trivial Pursuit is a Canadian invention. So are Balderdash, Pictionary, A Question of Scruples and Yahtzee. It may also interest you that Canadians have made their mark in the video game industry as well. And we've even figured out how to tastefully add a little "ooo-la-la" to the video world, in a controlled way, of course.

Trivial Pursuit

The story behind Trivial Pursuit—probably the first Canadian board game to take the world by storm—started just before Christmas in 1979, when *Canadian Press* sports editor Scott Abbott and his good friend, *Montréal Gazette* photo editor Chris Haney, challenged each other to a Scrabble duel to settle the argument of who was the better player. As often happens with disagreements, one thing led to another, and in this case, the friendly rivalry turned into a brainstorming session. In less than an hour, the two had come up with the premise and design of the game that became an "overnight sensation"—but if you ask its creators, a lot blood, sweat and money went into it. It took them another three months to figure out how to create the scoring rules for their new game.

After that, Haney quit his job and retreated to Spain with his brother John to research and write a collection of trivia for the game. Ed Werner, another friend, jumped on board, forming a four-man partnership. When the Haney brothers returned from Spain, the foursome started canvassing friends and family to jump on board financially. It costs a lot of money to produce a game—more money than the four of them could manage to scrape together on their own.

Once the money was in place, the first few packages rolled off the assembly line, and the partnership of Haney, Haney, Scott and Werner let out a collective sigh of relief. The concrete version of their creation had finally been produced, but there was a long way to go yet. There were game shows to attend and, hopefully, markets to tempt into ordering. The first 1100 games found homes in Canada quickly enough to give its inventors the courage to order more. They had 20,000 in storage when Trivial Pursuit made its debut at the American International Toy

Fair in New York City in February 1982. However, the orders they managed to attract at the fair fell far short of their goal. It started to look like even if they miraculously managed to sell the 20,000 games, they'd just break even if they were lucky.

They were lucky. The games that made it onto store shelves so enthralled game lovers that orders started pouring in. In 1984 alone, 20 million games were sold in the U.S. An article in the *New York Times* called Trivial Pursuit "A Party in a Box," and the rest, as they say, is history. Trivial Pursuit is one of 24 games named to the Games Hall of Fame.

Another Board Game First

Define the word "haustorium." Go ahead, you can do it, or at least try to make those sitting around the table with you think you can, which is the entire premise behind the board game Balderdash. Players pull up an obscure, never-before-heard-of word and write a definition of the word. When it's your turn, you have to choose the player who has the correct definition, and the best bluffer—because let's face it, how many of us can define "haustorium" anyway—is the one who gets the most points.

Laura Robinson, a London, Ontario-based actress, and her friend Paul Toyne invented Balderdash in the early 1980s, and it was first produced in 1984. The game is loosely based on The Dictionary Game, which was invented in 1971 and also plays with the idea of defining words. However, Robinson and Toyne pushed the idea into the bizarre category, making it a brainteaser as well as a lot of laughs.

The game received some criticism, if you can believe it. Some hurled accusations that the words used in the game don't actually exist—words such as "curupura," for example. According to the game, "curupura" means "a mystical bald one-eyed dwarf always seen riding a pig." But if you check the word out in any dictionary, online or otherwise, it's not there. (In the creators' defense, "curupura" could be a creature created by a fantasy writer somewhere.)

And in case you were wondering, the word "haustorium" is defined as "a projection from the hypha of a fungus into the organic matter from which it absorbs nutrients." And that, my friends, is according to good old *Webster*.

First Canadian-made Dice Game

We've all played it and pretty well know Milton-Bradley (now Hasbro) sells it, but I'll bet you had no clue Yahtzee was made in Canada. An unnamed Canadian couple who was a little bored and looking to liven up their yacht outing invented the game. Players roll five dice, trying to match one of the 13 pre-arranged configurations. For example, if they hit five of a kind, they call "Yahtzee!" and earn the highest individual score possible. After 13 turns, the person with the highest score wins.

Because they came up with the idea while on their yacht and had played it with their friends there for the first time, they initially called it The Yacht Game. The couple had such a good time playing it with their friends that about two years after coming up with the idea, they finally approached a toy manufacturer named Edwin S. Lowe to package and market the game. Lowe saw great possibilities in the game and quickly set out to get rights to it "in exchange for 1000 gift sets."

Because the inventors' names were not known, it's not clear if they ever knew of the game's great success. But all was not smooth sailing for Edwin Lowe. He changed the game's name to "Yahtzee" and tried to sell it, but it was a difficult game to explain to consumers and didn't take off at first. So Lowe developed a unique marketing plan. He decided to organize "Yahtzee parties" where people could experience the game firsthand. Lowe believed that consumers would only have to play a few rounds to be hooked, and he was right. Generations of Yahtzee players have bought and enjoyed the game with little more than word of mouth encouragement. The game's slogan is "The Fun Game That Makes Thinking Fun!" In 1973, Lowe sold his company to Milton-Bradley.

First Big Leap into Electronic Gaming

A leader in the Canadian electronic gaming industry is EA Sports, short for "Electronic Arts." From 1987 to 1992 the company had released several electronic game titles, including Earl Weaver Baseball, John Madden Football and NHL Hockey, which were all games for Sega Genesis and Nintendo game consoles. But then the company decided they'd take their vision a step further, developing sports game that created situations that were as lifelike as possible. Gamers could feel as if they were actually attending and participating in a sporting event. Designers created the EA Sports Network (EASN), used actual commentators such as John Madden to endorse the product, and in 1998 started producing NBA Live, FIFA, NHL, Madden NFL, and 2003 and 2004 models for NASCAR Thunder 2. EA Sports was among the first in the world of video gaming to focus on sport gaming in this way, and the company has released most of their videos for both PlayStation models.

Since 1993, the motto of EA Sports has been "It's in the game," and to ensure they're always the Most Valued Players in the gaming industry, the company usually releases a new game for each sport every season, and they've also expanded the repertoire of sports they cover.

Other Game Firsts

- 1984—Robert Simpson of Toronto developed the game Supremacy—a board game one source defined as a "game of warfare and economics among the world's super powers." It sold well, with 65,000 games making their way into gamesters' homes by 1992. You can now play the game online.

- 1985—Winnipeg's Henry Makow had his wits about him when he invented the board game A Question of Scruples, now known simply as Scruples and referred to by the company as "the game of moral dilemmas." The university professor's idea, which basically confronts players with a "what would you do" question in a number of suggested scenarios, sold like hotcakes, and today more than seven million copies of the game have sold worldwide.

- 1985—Fred Bates of Bates Games in Hamilton, Ontario, invented the board game Ultimatum. The Risk-type game has players battling it out to control the world. The game was fairly well received, selling 150,000 copies by 1992.

- 1986—*Toronto Sun* crime writer Max Haines developed the board game, An Evening of Murder, an interactive game where players are thrust into the middle of a preconceived murder and charged to solve it.

- 1986—Rob Angel of Vancouver, BC, developed the game Pictionary. The board game, loosely explained as "charades on paper," challenges players to draw images that other players have to guess at. The game was such a hit that it sold more than 15 million copies by 1992.

- July 1989—Torontonians Jerry Kuleba and Joe Shyllit come up with a humdinger of a game, called Humzinger, a world of warcraft card game. By 1992, 65,000 boxes of the game had already been sold.

- 1991—Everyone loves a jigsaw puzzle. But in 1990, Québec's Paul Gallant thought he'd take the idea and make the puzzle three-dimensional. It took some doing, but by 1991 the entrepreneur created his first prototype—the replica of a 1876 Québec-area mansion—and Wrebbit Inc. was well on its way to making puzzle history.

- 2005—If you're looking for a little adult adventure in your video game exploits, look no further than Lapis. Created by Ubisoft designer Heather Kelley, the game is geared to exploring female sexuality and is defined as "a magical pet adventure and a stealthy primer on female sexual pleasure." Players attempt to stimulate a response from a computerized bunny, but the same stimuli don't always receive the same response.

"Sex is a perfectly natural part of the human experience and there has to be a way to handle it meaningfully and tastefully in games," Kelley said after her Lapis prototype earned her first place at the Montréal International Games Summit in November 2005. The game is a first in its subject matter, but the international gaming industry expects consumers will see more of it.

Sports

*How would you like a job where, every time you make a
mistake, a big red light goes on and 18,000 people boo?*

–Jacques Plante (1929–86), hockey goalie

HUMANKIND HAS TAKEN part in sporting competitions for
centuries. Prehistoric cave art dating back to more than
30,000 years ago, for example, shows images of archery
challenges. Captain Cook's voyage to the Hawaiian Islands
in 1778 tells of the people there surfing. The Olympic
Games, generally considered the epitome of strength and
endurance testing, were established to develop a "sound
mind in a sound body" and started out in Olympia,
Greece, in 776 BC. By 394 AD they were banned, but in
1896 started up again internationally. And here in Canada, Native people have invented all kinds of physical
challenges. The Inuit used some of these activities, such
as tug-of-war and dogsled races, for example, to prepare
their youth for adult responsibilities.

Proving our physical prowess, whether it's against ourselves or anyone else, is part of many people's lives, and
Canadians, like people anywhere else in the world, are
devilishly competitive about their sports. Just think back
to the most recent Olympic Games and how eagerly even
the most disinterested among us waited for the latest
news on Canada's medal count. Although we don't rack
them up as quickly as countries like the U.S. and Russia—
we're a lot smaller, population-wise, after all—Canada
has a lot to be proud of when it comes to sports.

First Mega Marathons

The first man to run across Canada, from the eastern shores of North Sydney, Nova Scotia, straight through the more than 6200 kilometres to Vancouver was John (Jack) Gillis in 1906. A gifted and accomplished athlete, Gillis was inducted into the British Columbia Sports Hall of Fame in May 2006, and his accomplishment is something we can all admire. Whether Terry Fox, Steve Fonyo and other marathon athletes heard of Gillis before they too decided to traverse this vast country isn't known. Either way, each of these men have inspired a nation to rise above adversity and reach for the seemingly impossible.

Most Canadians know about Terry Fox, the young, 23-year-old cancer survivor from New Westminster, BC, who'd lost his right leg to osteogenic sarcoma, or bone cancer, and became the second Canadian to attempt a cross-country run. Fox had two main goals in mind: to raise awareness about the devastating affects of cancer and to raise money for research—he was aiming for one dollar from every Canadian. Terry set out on his nation-wide trek on April 12, 1980, at Cape Spear, Newfoundland, with the goal of running home—the promise of returning home is always a motivator.

During his run, his stump hurt and he grew tired, but never weary, until on September 1, 1980, it was clear he could run no longer. The cancer that had taken his leg had spread to his lungs. He had to stop his Marathon of Hope just outside of the city of Thunder Bay, Ontario, but by then he'd already reached one of his goals—even with his run cut short, he managed to raise a staggering $24.7 million for cancer research. On September 19 of that year, Fox accomplished another first when he became the youngest Canadian to be named a Companion of the Order of Canada. And his work inspired the world's largest, one-day fundraiser for cancer research with the Terry Fox Run, held each September.

Terry Fox died on June 28, 1981, but not before touching the heart of every Canadian old enough to remember his story.

One Canadian that especially related to Terry's life was 18-year-old Steve Fonyo. He too lost a leg to the same kind of cancer that took Terry's leg. And he too had a vision— he wanted to complete the work Terry began. And so on March 31, 1984, Fonyo embarked on his "Journey for Lives," retracing Terry's footsteps until he passed Thunder Bay and was blazing his own trail. After 14 long months of running, on May 29, 1985, Fonyo succeeded in completing Terry's dream when he arrived on the beaches of Victoria, BC, a spot that now bears the name Steve Fonyo Beach. Fonyo's trek marks the first cross-country fundraising marathon completed by one individual, and his efforts raised $13 million for cancer research. Fonyo was also awarded the Order of Canada in 1987.

Fonyo's success sparked enthusiasm for yet another fundraising effort. This time it was Rick Hansen who decided to raise money for research on spinal cord injuries. At the age of 15, Hansen was paralyzed from the waist down in a car accident, but that didn't stop him from tackling a marathon. His Man in Motion World Tour began in Vancouver, BC, as he started pushing his wheelchair across this vast country and beyond. He took him two full years to complete his journey, but in that time he clocked more than 40,000 kilometres across 34 countries and raised $26 million for spinal cord research in the process. He was also the "first student with a physical disability to graduate in Physical Education in the University of British Columbia." Hansen became a Companion of the Order of Canada in 1987.

Curling Firsts

When it comes to defining the origins of curling, many theories exist, but it appears the most widely held belief is that the sport started out in Scotland sometime in the 16th century. The game was first officially introduced into Canada in 1807, and the first curling club to set up operation was The Montréal Curling Club, which was founded in the same year, and after more than 200 years in operation, is "the oldest active athletic club in North America."

Originally, Scotland's Royal Caledonia Curling Club, founded in 1838, acted as the "mother club" for the Montreal club and others who started up. On March 6, 1935, a federal body, the Dominion Curling Association was formed as an administrative body for the men. In 1967 it evolved into the Canadian Curling Association, but it was still a men's sport club. Women interested in the sport formed their first official governing body, the Canadian Ladies Curling Association in 1961, and it wasn't until 1990 that the two groups amalgamated under the name Canadian Curling Association. Here are a few Canadian curling firsts:

- Although curling was first organized in Canada in 1807, it is commonly believed to have been introduced into this country even earlier. Some sources say the game was played in Québec City in 1759–60, and that cannonballs were melted to make curling stones.

- The Montréal Curling Club faced off against the Québec Curling Club in Trois-Rivieres in 1835. This marked the country's first "intercity game."

- Toronto Curling Club was formally organized in 1836.

- In 1838, the Royal Montréal Curling Club built an indoor rink. It was the first indoor rink in all of British North America.

- James Bicket of Toronto published the country's first official curling manual, *Canadian Manual on Curling* in 1840.

- Curling made it out west when Prince Albert and Battleford, Saskatchewan, both opened curling rinks in their respective communities in 1879.

- Alberta's first curling club opened in 1887 in Lethbridge, and the first club opened in BC, in Golden in 1894.

- Curling was already well established in Canada before the first women's club set up shop in 1894. Since women weren't admitted to the Royal Caledonia Curling Club in Scotland, the Montreal Ladies Curling Club made history in this country and their formation may have signified a world first.

- Canada's first Brier was sponsored by Macdonald Tobacco and took place in 1927 at Toronto's Granite Curling Club. Macdonald Tobacco sponsored the tournament until 1980, at which time Labatt took over the responsibility. Nokia Canada sponsored the event from 2001 to 2004, and in 2005 Tim Hortons took over sponsorship, holding its first Brier in Edmonton, Alberta.

- Curling made its inaugural appearance as a medal sport at the Olympic Winter Games in February 1998. The Canadian women's team, skipped by the late Sandra Schmirler, earned the first ever-Olympic gold medal for the sport. The Canadian men's team, skipped by Mike Harris, earned a silver that same year.

Royal St. John's Regatta

Most of us have a vague understanding that a regatta is some form of boat racing, but do you know where it got its start? The first mention of a regatta being held on Quidi Vidi Lake, near St. John's, Newfoundland, showed up in *The Royal Gazette* on August 6, 1816. However, no official records of such an event turned up until 1818, marking that year as the official start date in Royal St. John's Regatta history as well as the date of the first-ever regatta held anywhere in North America. It's also considered the "oldest annual sporting event" on the continent.

Most sources point to the regatta as the invention of a fishing captain named Hockins. The man worked from a small town called Wivenhoe, near the eastern coast of England, and he organized a makeshift regatta some time in the early 1800s. Large yachts were usually raced, and the rivalry between neighbouring fishing communities spurred on the event and helped make it popular. That said, there is some evidence that the Royal St. John's Regatta was held even earlier, beginning some time in the 1700s, with everything from gigs (small, light-built sail or rowing boats) and whale boats to jolly-boats (medium-sized boats belonging to a ship) being used.

The vessels used in a regatta have fixed seating for six team members: five rowers and a navigator, or coxswain. Men's races are 2.450 kilometres in length, and the women's races are 1.225 kilometres.

The regatta was conferred with the "Royal" prefix in 1993, but members of the Royal Family have been recorded as visiting the event as early as 1860.

Royal St. John's Regatta Trivia

- The Royal St. John's Regatta is "the only civic holiday in North America to be declared by a committee of persons not associated with a government body."

- The event, which takes an entire day to complete, is usually held on the first Wednesday of August. The regatta necessitated the establishment of a civic holiday because it drew a crowd of as many as 50,000 people, and anyone who knows Newfoundland knows that folks travel a great distance to take in the event. It is also the only known civic holiday that can be cancelled due to inclement weather.

- The regatta is also "one of the last fixed seat rowing competitions known to exist in the world."

Lacrosse

Long before our founding fathers first explored this great land, the Native people of Canada had a hand in developing some of our favourite sporting events. Take lacrosse, Canada's first real team sport, for example. Hundreds of years ago, Native people gathered in large groups, sometimes forming teams of 100 players, to challenge each other to a game some called *baggataway* or *tweaara-thon*, which translated means "Creator's game," so named because they believed the game was a gift from the Creator. Using metre-long sticks equipped with a pouch made of dried animal gut on one end, members of one team would catch and toss a ball made of deerskin, attempting to make their way through their opponents' teammates and score.

Early European settlers certainly approved of the game, and by the mid-1800s, French missionaries were even getting in on all the action. It was these missionaries who renamed the game "lacrosse," because they thought the stick used to play the game looked like a bishop's staff.

Dr. William Beers formally organized lacrosse in 1856, forming one of the country's first non-Native clubs when he established the Montréal Lacrosse Club. The Montréal-area dentist devised a formal set of rules and limited team sizes to 12. Lacrosse was named Canada's National Summer Sport on May 12, 1994.

246

CANADIAN FIRSTS

Other First Nations
Contributions to Sport

- Native people used sport as a way to build endurance and to test the limits of their youth, preparing them for their future as hunters and protectors. Some of these games were tug-of-war, spear throwing, dogsled racing, post and ring games such as ring toss, and arm and finger wrestling.

- Playing cards made from birch bark and dice games were also regular pastimes for Canada's early Native people. Sometimes players placed bets on their abilities at these and other games, which was used as a method to "redistribute surplus goods."

- One of the favourite games played by the Cree people was shinny. Similar to the game of hockey, shinny was played with long sticks, with or without a curved end, and a small ball that teams would compete to gain control of. Body contact with the ball was absolutely forbidden, and teams played for prolonged periods without a break.

- Double ball, or We Pitisowewepahikan, was another favourite among the Cree. In this baseball-type game, long sticks about a metre in length were used, along with two balls made with deerskin, stuffed with buffalo hair, and joined together with a strip of leather. Players were not allowed to touch the ball, and the ball was constantly passed from team member to team member by throwing it with their stick. The aim of the game was to toss the ball over the opposing team's goal line.

- The North American Indigenous Games, a large-scale sporting event, started out as a vision and a small gathering of 3000 people in 1971. That year, Enoch, Alberta,

hosted a 13-sport event for indigenous athletes, and it
spurred on the vision of holding a much larger games,
casting a wider net as far as participants went. By 1975,
the vision was accepted by Canadian and American
indigenous peoples, and in 1977 the Annual Assembly
of the World Council of Indigenous Peoples furthered
that vision by supporting the idea of hosting international games. The first such games were held in Edmonton, Alberta, in 1990.

First in Basketball

How do you keep a group of unmotivated and slightly unruly men happily occupied during an indoor gym class in the dead of winter? That was the problem facing 30-year-old James Naismith when he was challenged by his colleagues to come up with an activity that would interest a group of men in secretarial studies—callisthenics just didn't cut it with these guys. Naismith was used to challenges—this one led to an internationally popular game first developed by a Canadian. Having already completed three degrees, Naismith was anxious to begin his medical studies. In the meantime, he taught physical education at the Springfield, Massachusetts YMCA. But this particular group was a little more challenging than most, and he knew he had his work cut out for him.

For some time now, a game he had played when he was a youngster in Almonte, Ontario, got him to thinking. Called "Duck on a Rock," the game involved placing a fist-sized rock on a much larger boulder, and players took turns trying to hit the stationary rock off its perch using another fist-sized rock. He liked the game because it challenged him both physically and skill-wise, and it wasn't rough and potentially dangerous like indoor soccer or football.

From these rudimentary beginnings, Naismith crafted a new team sport. He used a ball about the size of a soccer ball. Two teams would vie for the ball with the goal of tossing it into a box attached to the wall on both ends of the gymnasium and placed high enough to tower above the players' heads. When two boxes large enough to accommodate the ball couldn't be found, two peach baskets were used instead. And from that serendipitous decision spawned the name basketball.

When he first unveiled his idea to his class, Naismith saw the doubt in the men's eyes, but any worries he had vanished as soon as he tossed the ball into the basket. The men took to the game, and pretty soon, spectators began stopping by to watch.

The first official basketball game ever held attracted more than 100 spectators, other athletes started up teams of their own, and before Naismith knew it, he'd made history.

As more games were played, modifications were made. It was a pain to climb a ladder to retrieve the ball every time someone scored, and so someone decided to cut out the bottoms of the peach baskets. Recognizing that his new sport was gaining popularity, Naismith sat down and wrote up the original 13 rules of play. And on December 21, 1891, just a few months after accepting the challenge of creating an indoor team game, basketball was officially born. Naismith may have eventually become an American citizen, but he was always proud of his Canadian roots. Canada was proud of him too.

First Goalie Mask

Talk about a demanding job. After seven years as net-minder for the Montréal Canadiens, Jacques Plante had suffered a broken jaw, shattered cheekbones, four broken noses and, after receiving 200 facial stitches, it was amazing his handsome mug didn't look more like a road map. But on November 1, 1959, he'd had enough. Like other goalies in the early days of hockey, Plante crafted himself a facemask for protection during practice, but no goalie ever wore such a contraption during a league game. It didn't matter to Plante. He'd just taken another puck in the face, earning him seven more stitches. This time he'd stand his ground. Either he'd go back on the ice with his facemask, or his team would play out the rest of the game with an empty net. Habs coach Toe Blake may not have liked the idea, but he didn't really have a choice in the matter. In giving Plante the green light, the Habs and their goalie made history when Plante wore a mask during a regulation game for the first time.

Plante continued to make history when, contrary to what everyone thought, the mask didn't inhibit his play, and he led his team to a 3–1 victory against the New York Rangers that November night. He never played another game without it.

The plastic mask Plante wore at first was fashioned by a sympathetic fan who knew of his many injuries. The mask didn't give Plante the full protection he was looking for, but it was a start. A few years later, another Habs fan by the name of Bill Burchmore, using his expertise working for a fibreglass company and coaching children's hockey, showed Plante his own idea for a goalie mask. At first, Plante resisted Burchmore's request to make a mould of his face, but he finally agreed, and after he used the finished mask, Plante knew eventually the world of hockey would follow his lead.

The first year Plante used his goalie mask, he recorded his lowest goals-against-average ever, and the mask became his signature piece.

Aside from the mask, Plante contributed a few other firsts to hockey history. He was "the first goalie to skate behind the net to stop the puck" and the first to alert his defenseman to an icing call by raising his arm above his head. He also penned the book, *Step by Step Hockey Goaltending*, making him the first goaltender to write a book on his profession.

Bowling Firsts

After a child's grave dating back to 3200 BC was discovered containing artifacts that looked like those belonging to the game of bowling, some historians believed the sport had been around for 5000 years. Sir Flinders Petrie dates the game of bowling back even further, to 5200 BC, after he discovered bowling pins and balls in an Egyptian tomb. Others, like German historian William Pehle, believe the game was invented in Germany in 300 AD. But it wasn't until 1366 that a written record of the game being played in England was discovered.

Regardless of its actual origins, or the many influences adopted from countries around the world with similar games, there are aspects to bowling that are uniquely Canadian. By the 1880s the Americanized form of 10-pin bowling made its way to Canada and was eagerly accepted by a population looking for a little leisure. Thomas Ryan established what is considered to be the country's first regulation 10-pin lanes in downtown Toronto. But his upper-class clientele complained that the balls were heavy and the game too strenuous, so Ryan had his father reduce the size of the balls, and Ryan reorganized the 10-pin setup to a five-pin one. And in 1909, Ryan introduced his modified game to an eager public. Ryan established the first five-pin bowling league the following year. Thomas Ryan passed away on November 19, 1961, and was inducted into Canada's Sports Hall of Fame in 1971.

Other Bowling Firsts

- Alfred Shrubb of Toronto played the first perfect game on record in 1918. At that time, a perfect score was 400.

- Toronto's Bill Bromfield scored the first perfect 450-point game in 1921.

- The women got in on the action when Marion Dibble started up the country's first all-ladies league in Toronto in 1921.

- The game of five-pin moves west to Winnipeg in 1923, making it the first league in Western Canada.

- The Canadian Bowling Association was established in 1927 and printed its first *Official 5-Pin Rule Book* in 1928.

- The game was adapted for the visually impaired, and the first blind bowling league was formed in 1935.

- Toronto's Tillie Hosken recorded a first for women when she scored a perfect 450-point game in 1940.

- Prior to 1957, when the first "automatic pin setting machine" was introduced, pins had to be set up by hand.

- In 1977, the Ontario Winter Games included five-pin bowling on their roster of competitive sports for the first time.

- In 1980, Canada faced off against a Filipino team in Manila, competing for the first-ever International Bowling Cup.

- The Canada Winter Games adds five-pin bowling to their list of competitive sports in 1983.

- In 1990, competitive bowlers were granted permission to use their personal bowling balls in competition.

- Canada's first national youth championship, the Canadian Youth Challenge Championship, was held in Hull, Québec, in 1998.

- Of course not all bowling games are played indoors. Since ancient Egypt, a form of lawn bowling was played, but of course it was a long time before the sport migrated to Canada. The first-ever lawn-bowling green constructed in this country saw its first games in the late 1880s in Nova Scotia at the Annapolis Royal garrison. Canada's first lawn bowling tournament was held in Toronto in 1888. By then there were at least seven lawn bowling clubs in the country since that many competed at the tournament.

- Women lawn bowlers formed their own organization in 1971. That's when the Canadian Ladies' Lawn Bowling Council was organized. Before then, women interested in the sport were affiliated with the Canadian Lawn Bowling Council. Still, men and women held their national championships concurrently.

- In 1999, Lawn Bowls Canada, which by then represented an amalgamation of men's and women's bowling leagues, was renamed Bowls Canada Bouligrin, which, according to the *Canadian Encyclopedia*, was an effort to better represent the different surfaces used to play the sport (indoor carpet and short mat, not just an outdoor lawn).

The World's Fastest Cyclist

Today's multiple-speed, lightweight, high-performance and durably built bicycle has come a long way from its roots as the "hobby horse." The first bicycle, built by Baron von Drais in Paris in 1817, was made of wood and certainly far less comfortable than the ergonomically correct versions put out today.

From their first appearance, bicycles have captivated the imagination of youngsters everywhere. Victoria's Sam Whittingham was no different. An avid cyclist all his life, Sam has taken the sport to new heights, breaking new records yearly for speed and endurance. He's the first person to power a bicycle under his own steam and reach speeds of 130 kilometres per hour—a record he set in 2002. And his endurance record of 86.752 kilometres in one hour has yet to be bettered.

Although he achieved his records with his own two legs, so to speak, he has a mighty fine set of wheels to help him along. Combining his love for bicycles with his skills as a theatrical set designer, Whittingham came up with the blueprints for the creation of the world's first Naked Bike—a bike equipped with a slick, bullet-shaped shell that helps cut through any wind resistance. He came up with his first design more than 30 years ago and has turned his lifelong love into a full-time business located on BC's Quadra Island.

Other Sporting Firsts

- It was 1900 before women were allowed to compete in the Olympics. Although it wasn't until 1924 that Canada sent its first female athlete, 15-year-old figure skater Cecil Eustace Smith, the year 1900 was still an important date in Canadian sports history. It was the first year Canada sent anyone to the Olympics. Two men, George Orton and Ronald J. MacDonald, competed in their respective events. Orton became the first Canadian to ever win an Olympic medal with a first-place finish in the 2500-metre steeplechase. He also earned a second medal, a bronze, in the 400 metre hurdles. MacDonald ran the marathon, but didn't place in the medals.

- The first competition of what we now know as synchronized swimming was held in Montréal in 1924. Details of the history of the sport are somewhat blurred, but it is believed ballet maneuvers were performed by swimmers in ancient times. However, Canadians played a huge role in developing the sport as we know it today. While practicing for their Royal Life Saving Society diplomas in the early 1920s, a group of Canadian women developed what they called "fancy swimming." Margaret (Peg) Sellers, a water-polo player and diver, took an immediate interest in the sport, and in 1938 she devised a standard set of rules. In the 1940s, "fancy swimming" became synchronized swimming, the sport debuted in the Olympics in 1952 and became an official addition to the roster in 1984.

- You don't have to tell a Calgarian this, but the rest of Canada might not know that the annual Calgary Stampede is known as "The Greatest Outdoor Show on Earth." The Calgary Exhibition was held in 1866, but it wasn't until the arrival of a cowboy named Guy

Weadick that the "Wild West Show" component was added to the show. The first Calgary Stampede was held in September 1912, and in 1923, the two events joined together to become the "Greatest Outdoor Show on Earth."

- Elizabeth Arden, founder of the cosmetic empire, became the "first woman owner in history to win the Kentucky Derby with her thoroughbred Jet Pilot."

- The Edmonton Commercial Graduate Basketball Team played from 1915 to 1940, and in that time this women's team established themselves as the most successful team in the sport's history. During their entire 25-year career, the team clocked 502 wins and 20 losses, with their longest winning streak running an incredible 147 games.

- In 2002, 26-year-old Calgary native Tyler Seitz made Canadian sports history when he became the first Canadian man to win a World Cup medal in the luge. His combined, two-run total of 1:29.286 was good enough to earn him a bronze medal.

- The first hockey player to record a 50-goal season was Montréal's Maurice Richard. He set the record during the 1944–45 hockey season. Richard was also the first hockey player to score more than 500 goals in his career; he retired in 1960 with 544 goals.

- The first swimmer to tackle Lake Ontario and make it all the way across was 16-year-old Marilyn Bell. She clocked the feat in 1954, and followed it up with another impressive record the next year as the youngest person to swim the English Channel.

- The first woman figure skater in the world to complete a triple Salchow was Petra Burka. She was just 15 years old in 1962, the year she managed the feat.

- In 1947, Canada's darling, Barbara Ann Scott became the first North American to win the European and World Figure Skating Championships. She also chalked up a number of other firsts. At just 13 she was the first female to ever land a double Lutz in competition. And in 1948 she was also became the first Canadian to win a gold medal in her sport during the Winter Games that took place in St. Moritz, Switzerland.

- Believe it or not, it wasn't until 1981 that a woman was elected to the Canadian Olympic Association. Abby Hoffman earned that coveted spot, and the same year also became the "first woman director general of Sport Canada."

- Elaine Tanner was just 15 years old when she made Canadian sports history in 1966. The swimmer competed at the Commonwealth Games and became the first person to walk away with four gold medals. In 1968 she chalked up another milestone, this time for winning three Olympic medals—two silver medals in individual events and a bronze in the relay.

- Twin sisters Sharon and Shirley Firth donned their cross-country skies and competed in the 1972 Olympics, making them the first Canadian Aboriginal women to do so. They went on to compete in three more winter Olympics and were the first women to compete in the Winter Olympics four consecutive times.

- Sue Holloway certainly earned her spot in Canada's Olympic Hall of Fame. In 1976, she became the first woman and first Canadian to compete in both the summer and winter Olympics. She cross-country skied for the winter event and boarded her kayak for the summer games.

- Clara Hughes earned two bronze medals in cycling in the 1996 Summer Olympics and a bronze medal in speed skating in the 2002 Winter Olympics, making her the first Canadian to win medals at both summer and winter games.

- The world of professional hockey saw the debut appearance of a woman goalie in 1992. That's the year Manon Rheaume strapped on the pads and played in goal for the Tampa Bay Lightning.

Notes on Sources

Websites

The following are among the many organizations, companies, individuals and government departments with Internet sites that provided valuable information in this collection. Any errors or omissions in the list are unintentional.

10 Downing Street

Africana Online

Agriculture and Agri-Food Canada

Alberta Energy

Alberta Heritage

Alpine Club of Canada

Andrew Bonar Law

Archives of Ontario

Athabasca University

Atlantic Cable

Avro Arrow

BabyTrekker

Bay of Fundy—Hopewell Rocks

Bick's Pickles

Birchwood Art Gallery

Blissymbolics

Byward Market

Canada Online

Canada Post

Canada's Fishery

Canada's Historic Places—A Federal Provincial Territorial Collaboration

Canadian Air Force

Canadian Children's Rights Council

Canadian Curling Association

Canadian Encyclopedia

Canadian Forestry Association

Canadian Geographic

Canadian Heritage

Canadian Legal Information Institute

Canadian Medical Association Journal

Canadian Medical Hall of Fame

Canadian Press

Canadian Space Agency

Canadian Space Agency

Canation Tour Guide Association of Toronto

Canola Council of Canada

Capital Health Alberta

CBC News
City of North Bay
City of Toronto Archives
City of Vancouver Archives
Collections Canada
Constitution Acts
Correctional Service Canada
CTV News
Department of Justice Canada
Departments of Tourism for BC, Newfoundland and Labrador, Halifax, Terrace, Vancouver, Toronto
Don's Maps
Elections Canada
Encyclopedia Britannica Online
Fisheries and Oceans Canada
Frostfree Nosepumps
Ganong—Canada's Chocolate Family
Globe & Mail
Great Canadian Salt Solution
Great Lakes Tourism
Greenpeace
Hamlet of Fort Laird
HealthImaging.com
Heroines.ca
Hiram Walker Distillery Place
History of Saskatchewan Waterways
History-Magazine.com
Holiday Spot Plus
Innovations Canada
International Society for Neonatal Screening

Irwin Toy Company
Japanese Canadians Then & Now
Jim Dreyer
John Howard Society
Kraft Canada
Labatt Brewery of Canada
Lapis
Leons Furniture
Library and Archives Canada
Living Traditions—Museums Honour the North American Indigenous Games
Macleods True Value
Marianopolis College Department of History
McGill Journal
McIntosh Apple
Medpage Today
Mines Action Canada
Molson Canada
Montréal Gazette
National Institute of Diabetes and Digestive and Kidney Diseases (NIDDK)
National Microbiology Laboratory
National Parks Service U.S. Department of Interior
National Post
National Research Council of Canada
New York Times
Newfoundland and Labrador Heritage

Books

Biberstein, Rene. *Bathroom Book of Ontario Trivia*. Edmonton, AB: Blue Bike Books, 2006.

de Figueiredo, Dan. *Canadian Top 10 Lists*. Edmonton, AB: Blue Bike Books, 2007.

Drew, Dick. *The Canadian Achievers*. Vancouver, BC: Drew Publications, 1991.

Ferguson, Will. *Canadian History for Dummies*. Mississauga, ON: John Wiley & Sons, 2005.

Kearney, Mark, and Randy Ray. *I Know That Name!* Toronto, ON: Dundurn Press, 2002.

Murphy, Angela. *Bathroom Book of Canadian Trivia*. Edmonton, AB: Blue Bike Books, 2005.

Nader, Ralph. *Canada Firsts*. Toronto, ON: McClelland & Stewart Inc., 1992.

Smith, Barbara. *Bathroom Book of Canadian History*. Edmonton, AB: Blue Bike Books, 2005.

Wojna, Lisa. *Canadian Inventions: Fantastic Feats & Quirky Contraptions*. Edmonton, AB: Folklore Publishing, 2004.

Wojna, Lisa. *Bathroom Book of Canadian Quotes*. Edmonton, AB: Blue Bike Books, 2005.

Author Bio

Lisa Wojna

Lisa is the author of three other non-fiction books for Folklore Publishing—*Amazing Dogs, Canadian Inventions* and *Great Canadian Women*. She's also the author of five other non-fiction books and has co-authored more than a dozen others. She has worked in the community newspaper industry as a writer and journalist and has travelled all over Canada from the windy prairies of Manitoba to northern British Columbia and even to the wilds of Africa. Although writing and photography have been a central part of her life for as long as she can remember, it's the people behind every story that are her motivation and give her the most fulfillment.